KU-008-484

It CAN'T Be TRUE! ANIMALS!

Senior editor Ashwin Khurana
Senior art editor Rachael Grady
Editors Annie Moss, Georgina Palffy
Editorial support Ann Baggaley, Carron Brown
Designers Chrissy Barnard, Mik Gates, Kit Lane
Illustrators Stuart Jackson-Carter, James Kuether,
Kit Lane, Peter Minister, Simon Mumford,
Charlotte Prince, Simon Tegg, 358 Jon @ KJA-Artists
Creative retouching Steve Crozier
Picture research Deepak Negi
Jacket design Akiko Kato
Jacket editor Emma Dawson
Jacket design development manager Sophia MTT
Producer, pre-production Jacqueline Street-Elkayam
Senior producer Jude Crozier

Managing art editor Philip Letsu
Managing editor Francesca Baines
Publisher Andrew Macintyre
Art director Karen Self
Associate publishing director Liz Wheeler
Publishing director Jonathan Metcalf

Written by Andrea Mills
Editorial consultant Derek Harvey

First published in Great Britain in 2020
by Dorling Kindersley Limited
80 Strand, London WC2R 0RL

Copyright © 2020 Dorling Kindersley Limited
A Penguin Random House Company
10 9 8 7 6 5 4 3 2 1
001–310219–February/2020

All rights reserved.
No part of this publication may be reproduced, stored
in or introduced into a retrieval system, or transmitted
in any form or by any means (electronic, mechanical,
photocopying, recording, or otherwise), without the
prior written permission of the copyright owner.

A CIP catalogue record for this book
is available from the British Library.

ISBN: 978-0-2413-4068-4

Printed and bound in China

A WORLD OF IDEAS:
SEE ALL THERE IS TO KNOW

www.dk.com

It CAN'T Be TRUE!
ANIMALS!

CONTENTS

Skills and senses

Unbelievable bodies

Strength and speed

Homes and hideaways

Growing and breeding

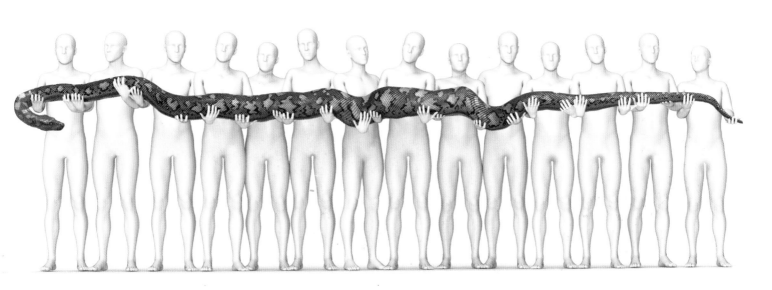

Skills and senses

Animals have incredible abilities that help them hunt, communicate, and keep safe. From sensing prey through electric signals to making and using tools, the animal kingdom is full of extraordinary creatures with a special skill or a super sense.

The basilisk lizard has an amazing talent for walking on water. When pursued by a predator, this lithe lizard uses its large, paddle-like feet to dash across the surface. It can travel in this way for up to 4.5 m (15 ft), covering 1.5 m (5 ft) a second.

How **far** can a shark **sense** prey?

Blacktip reef sharks are **expert hunters**, equipped with a **heightened sense** of smell that can detect prey over a distance of **1 km** (0.6 miles).

Blacktip reef sharks can **smell prey** as far away as the length of **six superyachts**.

The **blacktip reef shark** has quick reactions and a streamlined body to speed towards its prey.

The blacktip reef shark of the Indian and Pacific oceans uses its exceptional sense of smell to detect a drop of blood or fish oil in a volume of water 10 billion times greater. This is all the shark needs to move in on its prey at high speed.

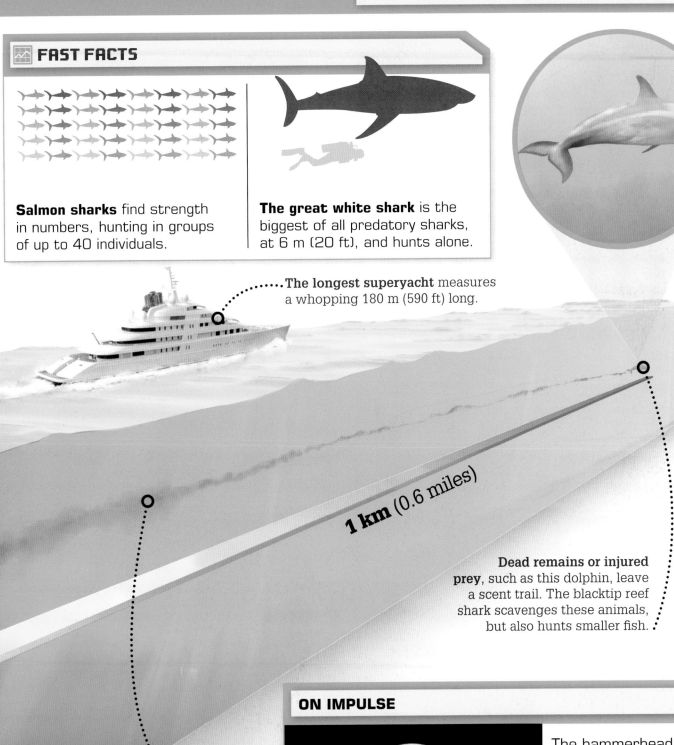

📊 FAST FACTS

Salmon sharks find strength in numbers, hunting in groups of up to 40 individuals.

The great white shark is the biggest of all predatory sharks, at 6 m (20 ft), and hunts alone.

The longest superyacht measures a whopping 180 m (590 ft) long.

1 km (0.6 miles)

Dead remains or injured prey, such as this dolphin, leave a scent trail. The blacktip reef shark scavenges these animals, but also hunts smaller fish.

Blood droplets can flow a long distance through the water, creating a perfect trail for the blacktip reef shark to find the injured prey. The blood from the injured prey thins to mere droplets over 1 km (0.6 miles) – just enough for the shark to detect.

ON IMPULSE

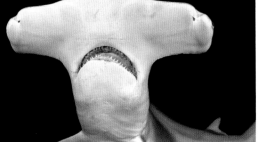

The hammerhead shark has sensory organs along its wide head that detect the electrical impulses of its prey. This helps the shark to locate prey, such as stingrays, that hide under the sand on the seabed.

2 m (6½ ft)

The water jet hits the insect with 10 times the force needed to topple it from its branch.

FAST FACTS

Some other animals have ways of catching prey that are as smart as the archerfish's sharpshooting.

The margay, a wild cat of the Amazon jungle, lures tamarin monkeys into pouncing distance by mimicking the cry of their infants.

A stoat puts on a display of leaping and "dancing" to hypnotize a rabbit, leaving it seemingly frozen to the spot and easy to kill.

Leaping stoat in white winter fur

Which fish shoots its prey with water?

The archerfish ranks among nature's most accurate hunters. This sharp-shooter targets unsuspecting prey by **squirting water** from its mouth with deadly speed and **precision**.

A jet of water squirted by the 20-cm (8-in) long archerfish, can be shot high enough to strike down its chosen insect from overhanging branches.

Hunting archerfish can squirt water to the height of 2 m (6½ ft).

HIGH JUMP

Archerfish have another technique for catching prey at close range. They leap right out of the water to snatch their victim, at times jumping twice their body length. This high-jumping hunting method is successful around 70 per cent of the time.

With their excellent vision, archerfish target their prey with great accuracy. When the victim falls, the archerfish takes a split second to work out where it will land, and is on the spot as the insect hits the water.

Most archerfish have silvery bodies marked with broad black bands. This colouring makes them hard to see when they swim near the surface.

Which ant explodes?

The **exploding ant** of Southeast Asia responds to enemy attacks by **sacrificing itself**. This **ultimate act** helps to **protect the ant's colony**.

If an intruder strikes, an ant of the *Colobopsis explodens* species – known as the exploding ant – is capable of ripping itself apart to release a sticky goo from inside its body. Although the exploding ant dies almost immediately, this aggressive action kills the attacker and protects the colony.

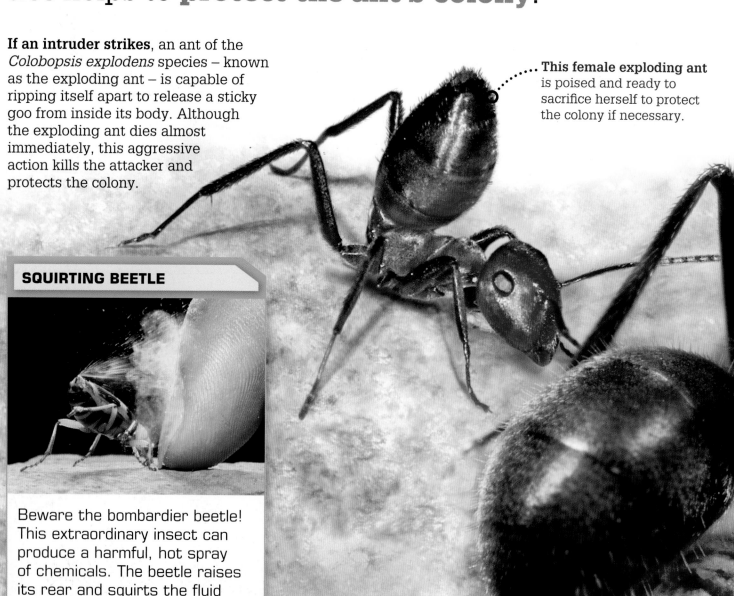

This female exploding ant is poised and ready to sacrifice herself to protect the colony if necessary.

SQUIRTING BEETLE

Beware the bombardier beetle! This extraordinary insect can produce a harmful, hot spray of chemicals. The beetle raises its rear and squirts the fluid from two glands at threats such as ants.

The attacking ant attempts to invade the exploding ant's colony to gain food and territory.

FAST FACTS

The exploding ant is just one of many insects with an unusual way to protect itself or its colony from attackers.

The red postman caterpillar has strong spikes and warning colours to deter attackers.

Toxic foam from the head of the koppie foam grasshopper stops enemies coming close.

The sharp, thorny appearance of thorn bugs makes them unappealing to hungry birds.

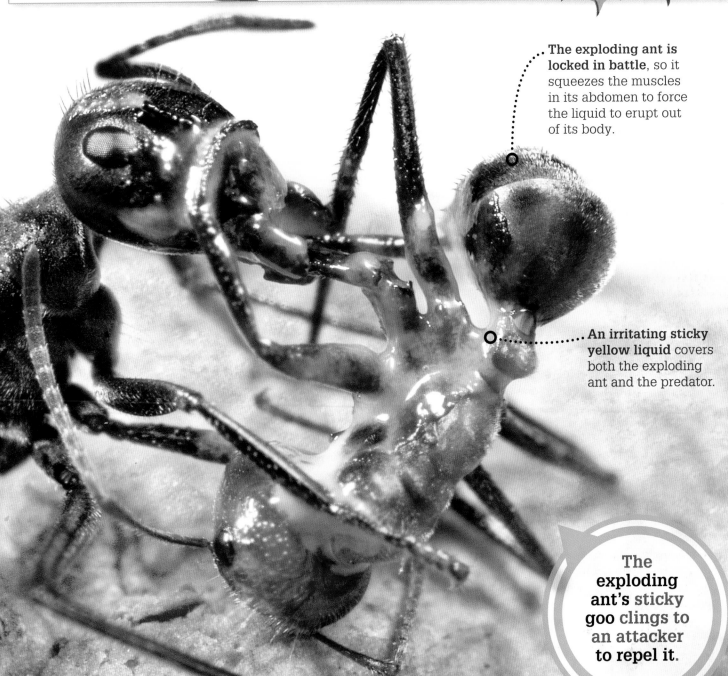

The exploding ant is locked in battle, so it squeezes the muscles in its abdomen to force the liquid to erupt out of its body.

An irritating sticky yellow liquid covers both the exploding ant and the predator.

The exploding ant's sticky goo clings to an attacker to repel it.

Why do skunks make a stink?

Predators beware! Skunks **kick up a stink** if an enemy comes close. Their **secret smelly weapon** is a **defensive spray** so disgusting that attackers are repelled instantly.

The skunk lifts its tail high if it feels cornered, then squirts the foul-smelling spray from glands in its bottom – aiming at the face of the predator.

The skunk's distinctive black and white fur warns potential predators to stay away.

The skunk's **stinky spray** **can reach a** target **3 m** (10 ft) away.

Scent glands beneath a skunk's tail produce an oily secretion with a strong smell of rotten eggs. The skunk can fire this fluid up to six times in quick succession at predators such as foxes and coyotes.

The fox recoils from the stench and closes its eyes to protect itself from the fluid. The spray can cause temporary blindness, which helps the skunk to escape.

FAST FACTS

Skunks are not alone in the smelly stakes — other creatures also produce unusual aromas.

The binturong of Southeast Asia sprays urine that smells of buttered popcorn to mark its territory.

As its name suggests, the peppermint stick insect sprays a minty smelling fluid when it feels threatened.

Happy honeybees produce a smell like lemons, but their warning whiff smells sweetly of bananas.

The fox's fur retains the foul stench of the skunk's spray for a few days but will not be permanently harmed by it.

DRINKING TEARS

Deep in the Amazon rainforest, butterflies and bees gather to sip the salty tears of a caiman, a reptile related to the alligators. Sources of salt, a mineral vital to the insects' health, are scarce in the forest. The caiman's tears, which keep its eyes lubricated when it is out of the water, are a welcome find.

The beak of the pileated woodpecker is strong, sharp, and shaped like a chisel. This means the beak can easily break into the bark.

Long, strong talons dig into the bark and give woodpeckers a strong grip.

Which bird can peck through a tree?

The **pileated woodpecker**, native to North America, is such a **powerful pecker** that its beak can hammer through **an entire tree trunk**. These rapid drillers can peck up to **12,000 times** a day.

The **rhythmic pecking action** of the pileated woodpecker is used to find food and communicate with other birds — such as when attracting a mate. This woodpecker is one of more than 250 woodpecker species, many of which can be identified by their unique pecking sounds.

Hollows in the tree trunk allow the hungry woodpecker to reach insects and insect larvae inside the tree.

Pileated woodpeckers can peck a tree 20 times per second.

The woodpecker's striking crimson head and black plumage are used to signal to other birds.

FAST FACTS

Woodpeckers have long tongues that wrap protectively inside their skulls during pecking and can extend to catch insects inside the tree.

Tongue

Tongue wrapped inside skull

Tongue

Tongue extended to catch an insect

What animals have **fingerprints** like a **human?**

Koalas and **primates** have fingerprints almost **identical** to ours, with strikingly similar **whorls and ridges**. Just like humans, every fingerprint has a **unique pattern**.

All the fingers of the human hand and the entire palm are covered in ridges.

Human

SPECIAL SNIFFER

Animals with hairless snouts, including dogs and cows, have unique nose prints. In fact, new computer software has been developed to identify any dog by its nose print.

Scientists would struggle to distinguish human fingerprints from those of primates and koalas. Primates, such as bonobos, have the same evolutionary history as us, but the koala's ridged fingerprints developed to grip onto eucalyptus trees and grasp leaves to eat.

Bonobo

The bonobo has similar fingerprints and the same hand structure as a human. This is because bonobos are primates, a group of related mammals that includes apes, monkeys, and humans.

Koala

Koalas have ridges on the fingertips and only parts of the palm. Even under a microscope they look almost the same as human fingerprints.

Fingerprints of humans, koalas, and primates are strikingly similar.

Using its beak and feet, the crow removes any leaves and bends the end of the stick into a hook shape.

New Caledonian crows are one of a few animals that design tools.

1. Scientists think the New Caledonian crow visualizes how to solve a problem before it starts making and using the tool. This crow finds and adapts a stick that can be used to hook insects from inside trees. In test conditions, these birds can even connect sticks together to make a longer tool.

📊 FAST FACTS

Smart bottlenose dolphins hold a sea sponge in their mouths to protect their rostrum (snout) from sharp rocks when they dive for food.

Sponge

Sea otters keep their favourite stone in a skin pouch, ready to break open the tough shellfish and clams they feed on.

Clam

Stone

The crow moves the stick up and down and from side to side in order to hook an insect.

2. The crow holds the adapted stick in its beak and pushes the hooked end into the bark or hole of a tree. An insect is caught on the hook.

Which **bird** is super **brainy?**

The **New Caledonian crow** is anything but a birdbrain. This **skilled species** uses its **beak and claws** to make and master **useful tools**.

Crows in the South Pacific islands craft tools in ways that were previously unknown in the animal kingdom. They are one of only a few creatures known to make tools to catch prey, saving them time and energy.

New Caledonian crows have large brains relative to their body size, which could be one of the reasons why they are so good at solving problems.

TOP DOGS

Although they don't make tools, service dogs are trained to use them to assist the disabled or to aid emergency rescues. This dog uses a rope to open a door for a man in a wheelchair.

3. Having hooked an insect with the tool, the crow drops the stick and grabs the insect with its beak. Often the crow will stand on the stick so it can use its tool again.

Antarctic krill can form huge groups, even bigger than locust swarms.

120 million
Antarctic krill

Hundreds of millions of tiny shrimp-like Antarctic krill turn the waters red with swarms several kilometres wide. Their swarms can even be spotted from space.

32 million
House mice

Crops are regularly ruined when swarms of several million mice inexplicably move across rural Australia roughly once every four years.

Animals form swarms for many different reasons. Antarctic krill pull together to prevent predators from singling out a target. Garter snakes swarm during mating season. Some animals, like red-billed queleas, join forces in search of food. The reason why house mice swarm, however, remains a mystery.

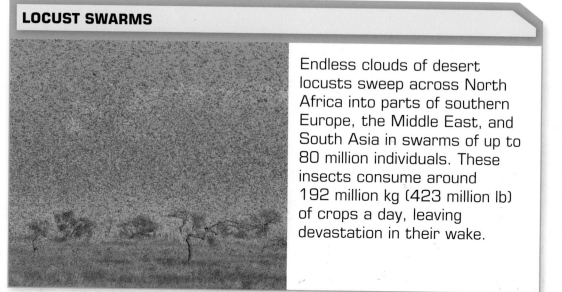

LOCUST SWARMS

Endless clouds of desert locusts sweep across North Africa into parts of southern Europe, the Middle East, and South Asia in swarms of up to 80 million individuals. These insects consume around 192 million kg (423 million lb) of crops a day, leaving devastation in their wake.

2 million
Red-billed quelea

African red-billed quelea flock in huge numbers to form unstoppable swarms. The birds target food crops, causing devastation for farmers.

75,000
Garter snakes

Rural Canada is home to thousands of garter snakes, which form large, knotted breeding swarms during mating season.

Are locusts the only swarmers?

Locusts are famous for their **plague-like swarms**, but animals such as **mice** and **birds** also mass together in huge groups to **migrate, breed, or feed**.

Caterpillars in fancy dress

Before they transform into **butterflies** and **moths**, **caterpillars** come in **wild designs** and **colours** that **warn** predators of the **dangers** of eating them.

Saddleback caterpillar
The saddleback wears its bright markings like a high-visibility jacket, sending out a "don't touch" message to predators. Spines at the caterpillar's front and rear pack an extremely painful sting. The brown moth that emerges from this astonishing caterpillar is surprisingly plain.

Puss moth
The adult moth is named for its fluffy-cat appearance. As a caterpillar, it uses its fierce face and whiplash tails as threats, but its real defence is to squirt acid.

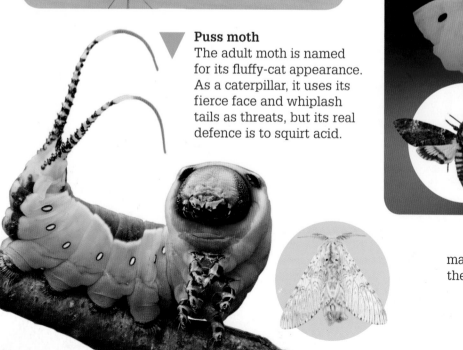

Death's-head hawk moth
This sinister name comes from the skull-like markings on the adult moth. No less impressive, the hefty yellow and green caterpillar may grow up to 12.5 cm (5 in) long. When threatened it will click its jaws to ward off predators, or even attempt to bite them.

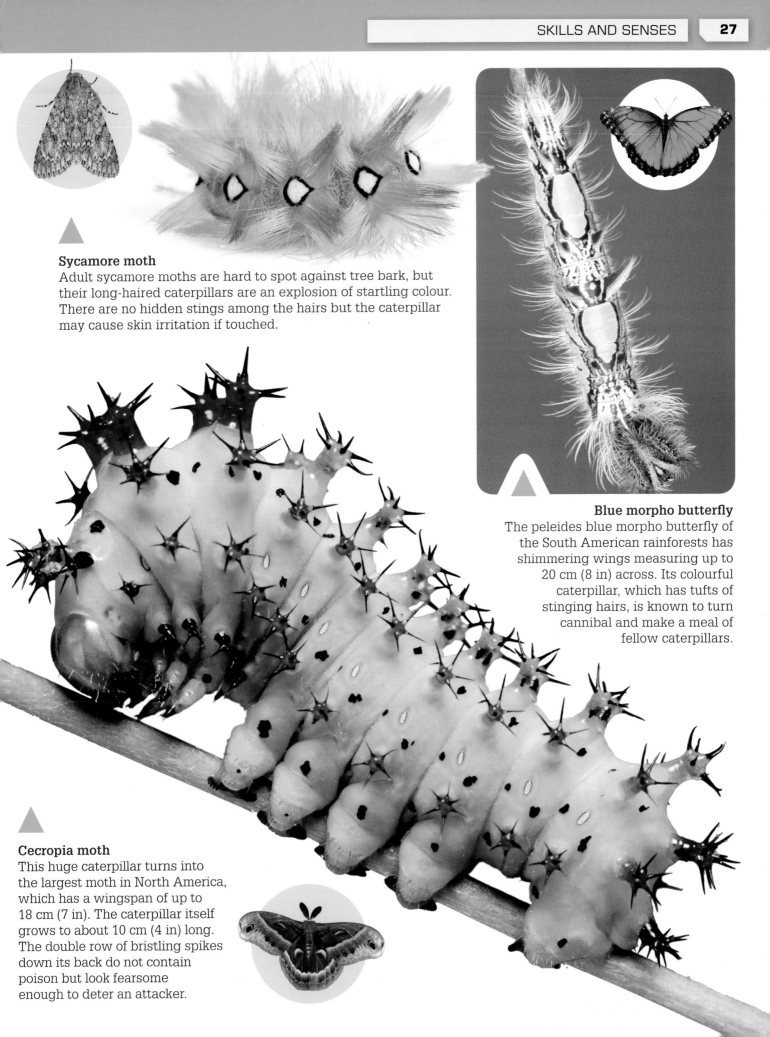

Sycamore moth
Adult sycamore moths are hard to spot against tree bark, but their long-haired caterpillars are an explosion of startling colour. There are no hidden stings among the hairs but the caterpillar may cause skin irritation if touched.

Blue morpho butterfly
The peleides blue morpho butterfly of the South American rainforests has shimmering wings measuring up to 20 cm (8 in) across. Its colourful caterpillar, which has tufts of stinging hairs, is known to turn cannibal and make a meal of fellow caterpillars.

Cecropia moth
This huge caterpillar turns into the largest moth in North America, which has a wingspan of up to 18 cm (7 in). The caterpillar itself grows to about 10 cm (4 in) long. The double row of bristling spikes down its back do not contain poison but look fearsome enough to deter an attacker.

FROM PREDATOR TO PREY

Along a riverbank in Brazil, a skilful jaguar turns a caiman — a fearsome predator to most other animals — into its prey. The jaguar hides on the shady bank waiting for the caiman to swim past. When the unsuspecting reptile is close, the jaguar leaps into the water with claws and teeth bared. The caiman is wrestled to the shore where the jaguar, with the strongest bite force of all the big cats, overpowers it in minutes.

How do whales sleep?

Most whales, like other mammals, sleep **horizontally**. However, the **sperm whale** is an exception: this supersize snoozer sleeps **upright** underwater.

This upright position is still a mystery to scientists researching the sperm whale's sleep habits.

These mighty mammals take power naps lasting no more than 15 minutes, while floating upright below the ocean surface. Sperm whales spend only 7 per cent of their lives asleep, a tiny amount compared to humans who spend nearly 33 per cent of their lives asleep.

Sperm whales close their eyes and remain entirely motionless while sleeping.

SKY-HIGH SLEEP

Some birds can sleep during flight by keeping one eye open and half their brain awake. The Alpine swift adopts this method to stay airborne for up to 200 days at a time.

Sperm whales can sleep upright at depths of 10 m (33 ft) beneath the surface.

Small pods of about five sperm whales come together for these short rests.

FAST FACTS

The koala dozes for 15 hours a day. Its low-energy, leafy diet only enables it to be active for a few hours each day.

Walruses can sleep in water by resting their head on floating ice or by filling their throat with air to keep them afloat.

Ostriches remain alert to danger by sleeping for only short spells and standing up for these naps, ready to run away from predators.

Rise of the chimps

Humans have always been fascinated by chimpanzees. They share 96 per cent of our DNA, and characteristics including high intelligence, recognizable facial expressions, and family living. These amazing animals can even learn words and solve problems. This appeal, however, has led to illegal trade. They are also threatened by habitat loss.

A key figure in efforts to protect chimpanzees is the British primate expert and conservationist Dr Jane Goodall. In 1960, she visited Tanzania and observed these remarkable primates adapting leaves, sticks, and twigs for hunting, feeding, cleaning, and fighting. This was the first time such incredible behaviour had been recorded, and it quickly gained public attention.

Chimpanzees in the wild, live in large communities made up of around 15 to 80 members.

Dr Goodall's observations, her conservation work, and contributions to environmental education have helped to protect this astonishing endangered species. Although there are around 250,000 chimps living in the wild today, their habitats still need much protection.

BACK · FROM · THE · BRINK

CONSERVATION

Sociable chimpanzees
These primates live in close family groups, and teach their young important life skills such as using tools.

LIFE ON LAND

Unlike most fish, mudskippers can walk on land for up to 90 per cent of the time. This is because they have modified fins for movement, hold mouthfuls of water to absorb oxygen, and can see clearly in air.

This rare fish is not a strong swimmer, so it uses four fins to walk on the sea floor when hunting for worms. This movement is similar to that of four-legged land animals.

Webbed fins propel the handfish slowly across the sand.

Flexible elbows help the handfish to walk on the uneven sea floor.

Which fish can walk?

One **remarkable species** makes waves in the coastal waters of Tasmania, Australia. While most other fish are swimmers, the **handfish walks** along the seabed with specially **adapted fins**.

Large fins stand up from the back and head to help the handfish move through the water.

A unique pattern of orange and brown spots and flattened warts adorn each handfish.

The **handfish** walks on four adapted fins that **resemble human hands**.

Adult handfish measure about 15 cm (6 in) long.

Underwater bristle worms make a tasty treat for this hungry handfish.

How far can a wolf howl?

The **howling grey wolf** is known for its night-time cries. Their **call of the wild** can be heard by other members of the pack up to **11 km** (7 miles) **away**.

A wolf in Central Park, could howl to another wolf at the end of Manhattan.

Howl

11 km (7 miles)

Lone wolves usually howl to make contact with their pack after going out hunting.

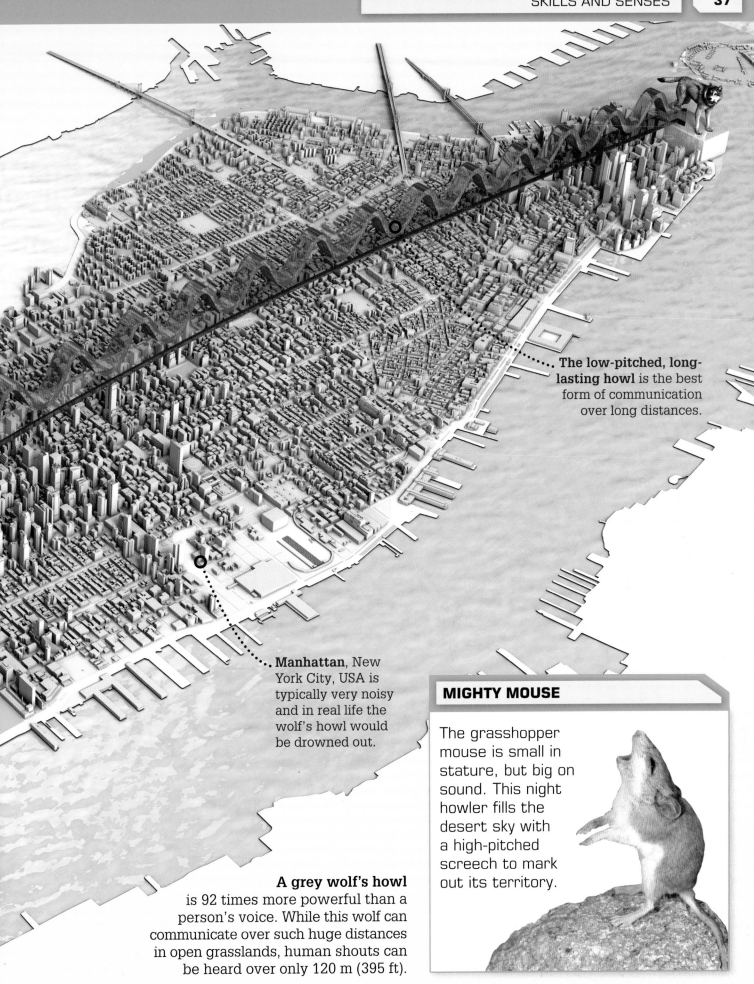

The low-pitched, long-lasting howl is the best form of communication over long distances.

Manhattan, New York City, USA is typically very noisy and in real life the wolf's howl would be drowned out.

MIGHTY MOUSE

The grasshopper mouse is small in stature, but big on sound. This night howler fills the desert sky with a high-pitched screech to mark out its territory.

A grey wolf's howl is 92 times more powerful than a person's voice. While this wolf can communicate over such huge distances in open grasslands, human shouts can be heard over only 120 m (395 ft).

With its streamlined body and waterproof fur, **the platypus** is a master hunter. This unusual mammal's most curious feature is the duck-like bill, which locates prey with absolute accuracy.

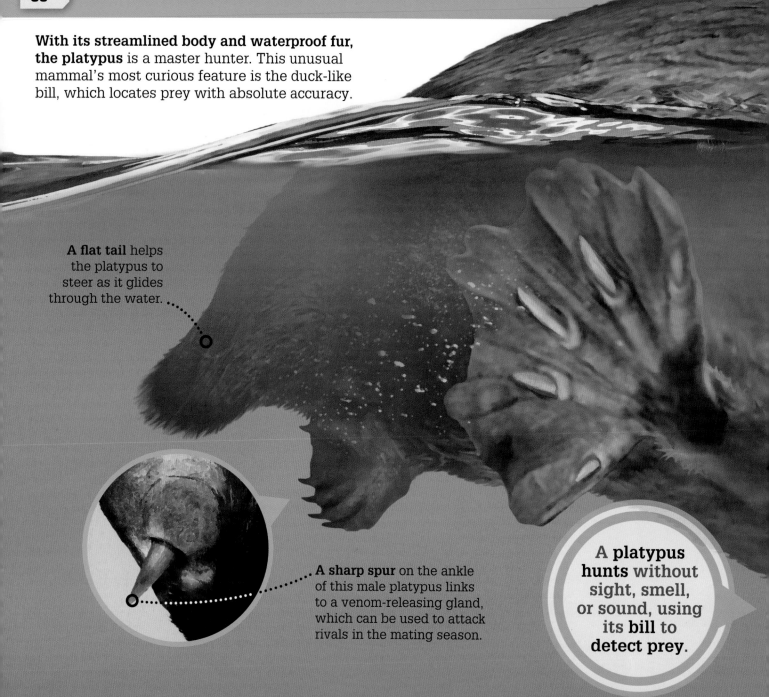

A flat tail helps the platypus to steer as it glides through the water.

A sharp spur on the ankle of this male platypus links to a venom-releasing gland, which can be used to attack rivals in the mating season.

A platypus hunts without sight, smell, or sound, using its bill to detect prey.

What **mammal** has a **duck-like bill?**

The **duck-billed platypus** uses extraordinary methods to find food, using its **super-sensory bill** to detect underwater prey.

Large front feet are webbed
and work like paddles to
propel the platypus through
the water towards its prey.

The bill has 40,000
tiny organs, called
electroreceptors,
that sense electric
currents made
by prey.

WARM EGGS

The platypus is one of
only two kinds of mammal,
along with the echidna,
that lay eggs. A female
platypus lays one or two
eggs in a burrow beneath
a river bank and uses
her body heat to warm
them until they hatch.
Here a scientist holds
two platypus eggs.

**When the platypus
is swimming,** its
nostrils and ears close
to keep water out.

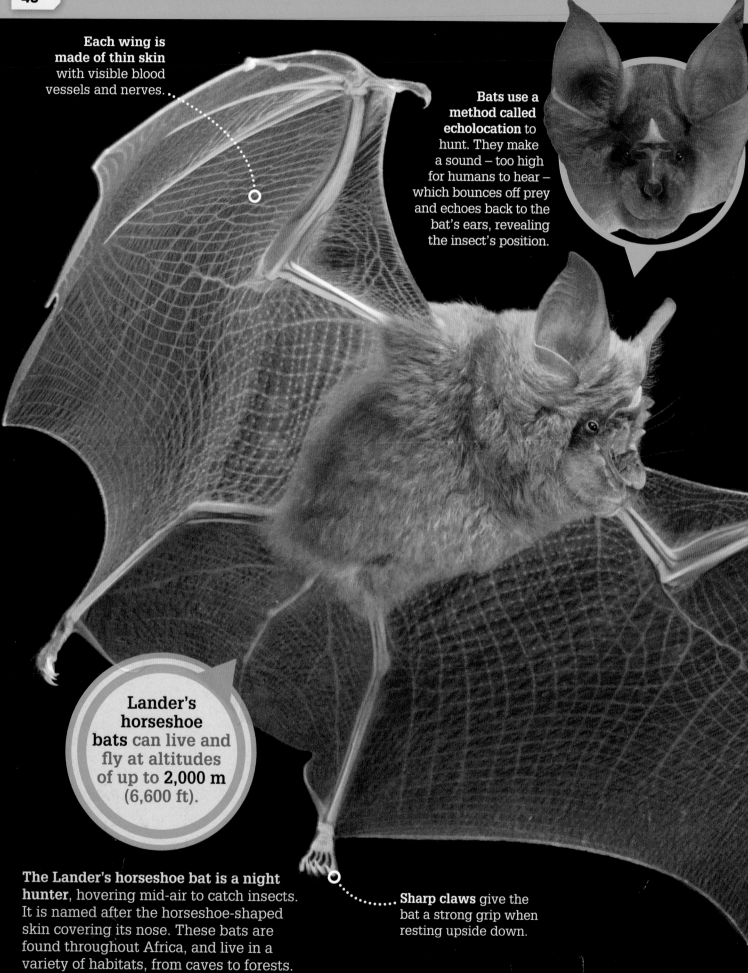

Each wing is made of thin skin with visible blood vessels and nerves.

Bats use a method called echolocation to hunt. They make a sound – too high for humans to hear – which bounces off prey and echoes back to the bat's ears, revealing the insect's position.

Lander's horseshoe bats can live and fly at altitudes of up to **2,000 m** (6,600 ft).

The Lander's horseshoe bat is a night hunter, hovering mid-air to catch insects. It is named after the horseshoe-shaped skin covering its nose. These bats are found throughout Africa, and live in a variety of habitats, from caves to forests.

Sharp claws give the bat a strong grip when resting upside down.

Which mammal can fly?

With their **powerful muscles** and **strong wings**, **bats** are the only mammals that have evolved the ability to **fly**. They **catch flying insects** using a skill called **echolocation**.

A bat's wings have lightweight bones with moveable joints that are more like those of a human hand than a bird's wing. These flexible joints allow bats to change direction suddenly when hunting prey.

Large moths make up almost the entire diet of the Lander's horseshoe bat.

HOME TO ROOST

Bats rest together in trees, caves, or crevices in gatherings called roosts. Bats hang upside down in the roost but never get dizzy because they are too small for gravity to cause a blood rush to their brain.

What animal is the **loudest?**

We all know someone with a **loud voice**, but these animals can **out-shout** most humans.

The screaming piha is the loudest bird of its 25-cm (10-in) size. It has a three-part song that it uses to attract a mate.

Screaming piha **112 dB**

Alligators and crocodiles let out loud bellows to attract mates.

American alligator **94 dB**

Human **129 dB**

Jill Drake from the UK holds the world record for the loudest scream by a person.

SNAPPING SHRIMP

The tiny pistol shrimp makes a huge sound, but not with its mouth. The shrimp snaps its claws so fast, the action creates a sonic boom as loud as 200 dB.

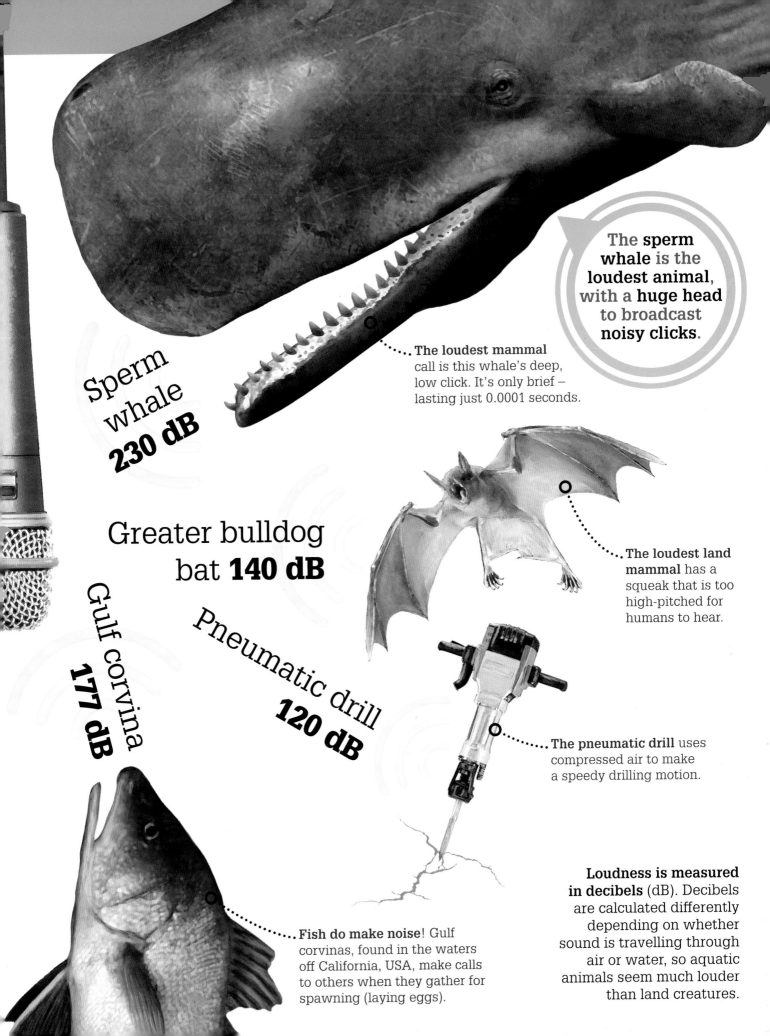

Sperm whale 230 dB

The sperm whale is the loudest animal, with a huge head to broadcast noisy clicks.

The loudest mammal call is this whale's deep, low click. It's only brief – lasting just 0.0001 seconds.

Greater bulldog bat 140 dB

The loudest land mammal has a squeak that is too high-pitched for humans to hear.

Gulf corvina 177 dB

Pneumatic drill 120 dB

The pneumatic drill uses compressed air to make a speedy drilling motion.

Fish do make noise! Gulf corvinas, found in the waters off California, USA, make calls to others when they gather for spawning (laying eggs).

Loudness is measured in decibels (dB). Decibels are calculated differently depending on whether sound is travelling through air or water, so aquatic animals seem much louder than land creatures.

Skills and senses facts

HIGHEST *JUMPING* ANIMALS

The animal kingdom is bursting with skilled springers that can leap to great heights. Here are six of the **world's best jumpers**.

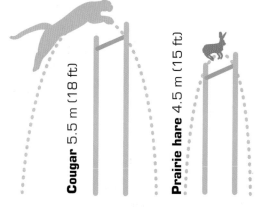

Cougar 5.5 m (18 ft)

Prairie hare 4.5 m (15 ft)

Spinner dolphin 3 m (10 ft)

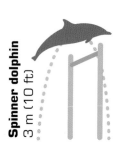

Impala 3 m (10 ft)

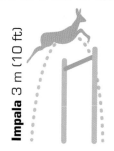

Red kangaroo 3 m (10 ft)

Kangaroo rat 2.75 m (9 ft)

LONGEST TIME IN FLIGHT

When **not breeding**, these amazing birds spend **long periods** of time in **continuous flight**.

X	X	X
X	X	X
X	X	X
10	11	12

◄ Common swift
This migratory bird can spend around **10 months per year** in the air, travelling up to 9,656 km (6,000 miles).

X	X	X
X	X	X
7	8	9
10	11	12

◄ Alpine swift
In flight for up to **six months per year**, the Alpine swift eats flying insects and airborne spiders.

X	2	3
4	5	6
7	8	9
10	11	12

◄ Frigate bird
When a juvenile, this seabird flies for up to **two months per year**, gliding on its 2.3-m (7½-ft) wingspan.

DEFENCE WEAPONS

Some small animals have **incredible** ways to **protect** themselves from larger predators.

The *Texas horned lizard* can squirt a **jet of foul-tasting blood** from its **eyes** straight into a predator's mouth.

Blood jet

The *Spanish ribbed newt* pushes its **ribs** out through its **skin** to form **spikes**.

Exposed rib

ANIMALS *THAT CHANGE* COLOUR

▲ Golden tortoise beetle
This beetle changes from **gold** to **red** when it is mating or threatened. This is caused by a **liquid secretion** that changes how the body **reflects light**.

▲ Seahorse
Seahorses have tiny sacs of **pigment** in their skin that is able to expand or shrink to make them **change colour** for **camouflage**.

▲ Pacific tree frog
Tiny sacs of **pigment** in the frog's skin make it **change colour** according to the **brightness** of light, helping it with **camouflage** as seasons change.

MOST SENSITIVE SENSE OF SMELL

Bears 32 km (20 miles)

Elephants 19 km (12 miles)

Moths 10 km (6 miles)

With their **super sense of smell**, these animals can **sniff out** a mate, threat, or food over **huge distances**.

LONG DISTANCE GLIDERS

A lack of wings doesn't stop these animals **taking off**! These **great gliders** spread their bodies and use **air currents** to sail through the skies.

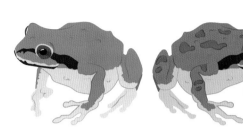

Red and white giant flying squirrel
400 m (1,312 ft)

Yellow-bellied glider
140 m (459 ft)

Flying fish
50 m (164 ft)

WALKING ON WATER

- **Basilisk lizards** can run across water up to **4.5 m** (15 ft) by trapping air under their **large fleshy feet** and pushing against the water's surface.

- **Water striders** are aquatic insects that have **hairy legs** that help them **skip across the water** without sinking.

- **Brazilian pygmy geckos** are small enough to drown in a raindrop, but they have **water repellant skin** that helps them **stand on water**.

Unbelievable bodies

Extraordinary animals throng the animal kingdom, each species adapted in a special way for its own survival. From slimy creatures of the deep to coconut-cracking crustaceans, many animals have truly unbelievable bodies.

The star-nosed mole is one of the world's strangest-looking animals. Its amazing star-shaped snout is a super sensor for this blind carnivore, helping it to detect prey as it tunnels through soil.

The tail fluke is up to 7 m (23 ft) wide, which is around a quarter of the whale's 32.6-m (107-ft) body length.

The blue whale is the world's heaviest animal. Even newborn whale calves weigh a whopping 2,700 kg (6,000 lb), which is roughly the same as an adult hippopotamus. A calf can gain 60 kg (132 lb) a day in the first year – almost as much as an average person weighs – guzzling 225 litres (50 gallons) of its mother's fat-rich milk daily. Female blue whales can weigh more than males.

A blue whale can weigh the same as **32 male Asian elephants**.

1 blue whale = 150,000 kg (331,000 lb)

A whale's pectoral fins, or flippers, are up to 4.8 m (15 ft 9 in) long. They help the whale to move in a specific direction.

FAST FACTS

The bee hummingbird is the world's smallest bird, weighing just 1.6 g (0.06 oz). It would take 37 of them to balance the weight of one fidget spinner.

An average fidget spinner weighs 59 g (2 oz), which is the same as 37 bee hummingbirds.

Up to 88 grooves stretch from chin to navel, allowing the throat to balloon out with water when the whale feeds.

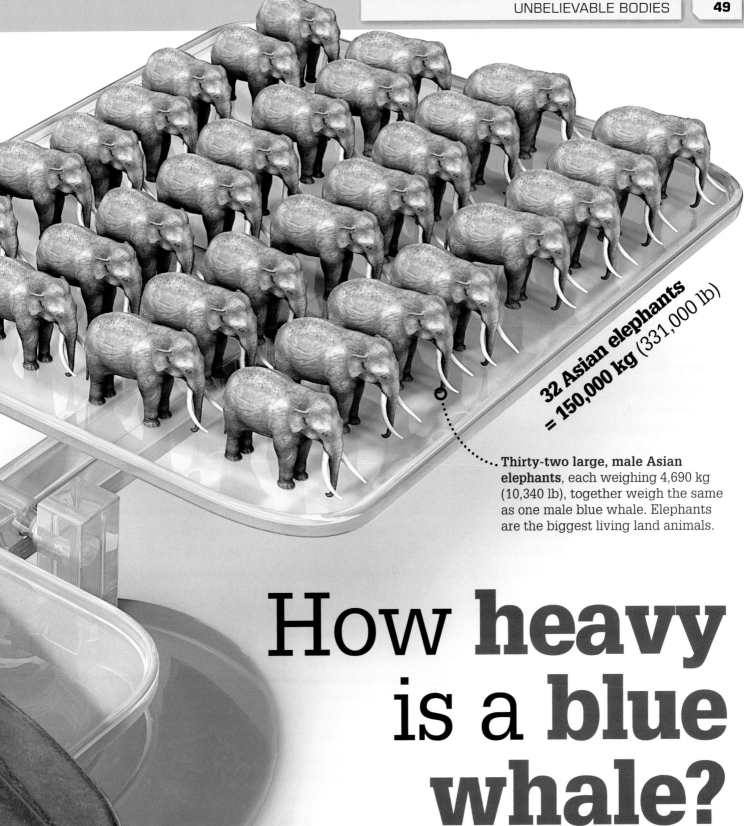

32 Asian elephants = 150,000 kg (331,000 lb)

Thirty-two large, male Asian elephants, each weighing 4,690 kg (10,340 lb), together weigh the same as one male blue whale. Elephants are the biggest living land animals.

How heavy is a blue whale?

Earth's largest animal, the **blue whale** can weigh up to **150,000 kg** (331,000 lb). Its **tongue** alone weighs as much as **an elephant**.

Which octopus is a master of disguise?

A **shape-shifter** lurks in tropical waters off the **Indonesian coast**. This is the **mimic octopus**, which **imitates** other sea creatures to **fool predators** or to get **close enough to prey** for a swift grab.

The mimic octopus copies the flounder's behaviour by hiding on the seabed.

The mimic octopus pulls its long tentacles close together to form a realistic flounder's "tail".

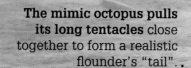

WARNING COLOURS

When not imitating other animals, the mimic octopus has a bold stripy pattern. These colours might be enough to startle would-be attackers, giving the octopus time to beat a hasty retreat.

Taking on a fish shape and changing its own markings to a mottled pattern, the mimic octopus becomes the flounder's twin.

The soft-bodied mimic octopus has no hard skeleton, so it can change shape with flexibility and ease. By also altering the colour, pattern, and texture of its skin, this clever octopus can turn itself into a flatfish, such as the flounder it is copying here, and give convincing impressions of many other fellow sea creatures (see Fast Facts).

FAST FACTS

A mimic octopus is said to imitate up to 13 other types of marine animal. Some of its tricks are shown here.

Sea snake   Stingray   Hermit crab   Lionfish

Mimic octopus   Mimic octopus   Mimic octopus   Mimic octopus

The flounder's blue spotted skin helps to make it less noticeable in the clear, sun-dappled waters.

All flatfish, like this flounder, have both eyes on one side of the head.

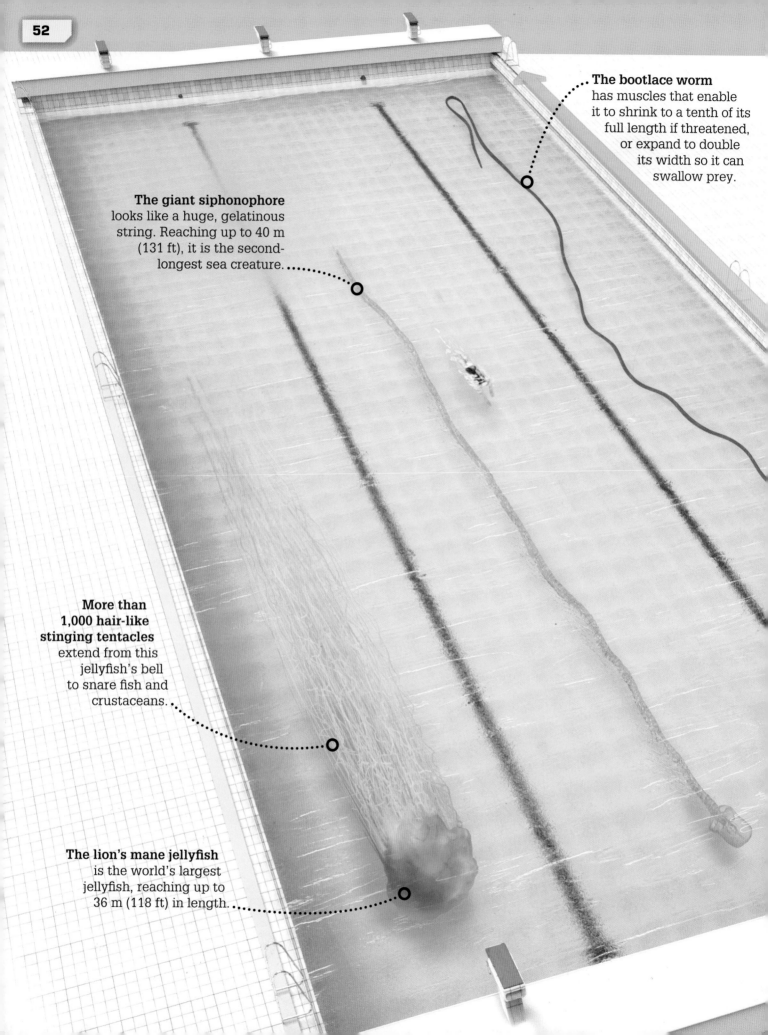

The bootlace worm has muscles that enable it to shrink to a tenth of its full length if threatened, or expand to double its width so it can swallow prey.

The giant siphonophore looks like a huge, gelatinous string. Reaching up to 40 m (131 ft), it is the second-longest sea creature.

More than 1,000 hair-like stinging tentacles extend from this jellyfish's bell to snare fish and crustaceans.

The lion's mane jellyfish is the world's largest jellyfish, reaching up to 36 m (118 ft) in length.

What is the longest animal?

Beneath the chilly waters of Britain's North Sea coast lives the **longest creature on Earth**. The **bootlace worm** is a wriggly whopper, measuring up to **60 m** (197 ft) in length.

A member of the ribbon worm family, the bootlace worm makes most other marine life look small, growing almost twice as long as the blue whale. It produces a powerful toxic mucus to kill crustaceans, but is unlikely to harm humans.

50 m (164 ft)

The bootlace worm is less than 1 cm (½ in) across – about the same width as a flat noodle.

The bootlace worm is **10 m** (33 ft) **longer** than an Olympic pool.

FAST FACTS

The dwarf lanternshark is the world's smallest shark. With the largest specimen measuring only 20 cm (8 in), most are shorter than an adult's hand is long.

18 cm (7 in)

The world's smallest jellyfish is Šivickis' Irukandji. Despite having a maximum bell height of only 1.2 cm (½ in) — the size of a jelly bean — it is highly venomous.

Šivickis' Irukandji jellyfish

Jelly bean

HUMAN-SIZED JELLYFISH

A huge barrel jellyfish was captured on camera by divers filming a documentary off the British coast. Also called a frilly-mouthed jellyfish, this sea creature has hundreds of little mouths on its frilly arms. This 1.5-m (5-ft) long animal feeds on tiny plankton. In warmer waters, it is the favourite food of leatherback turtles.

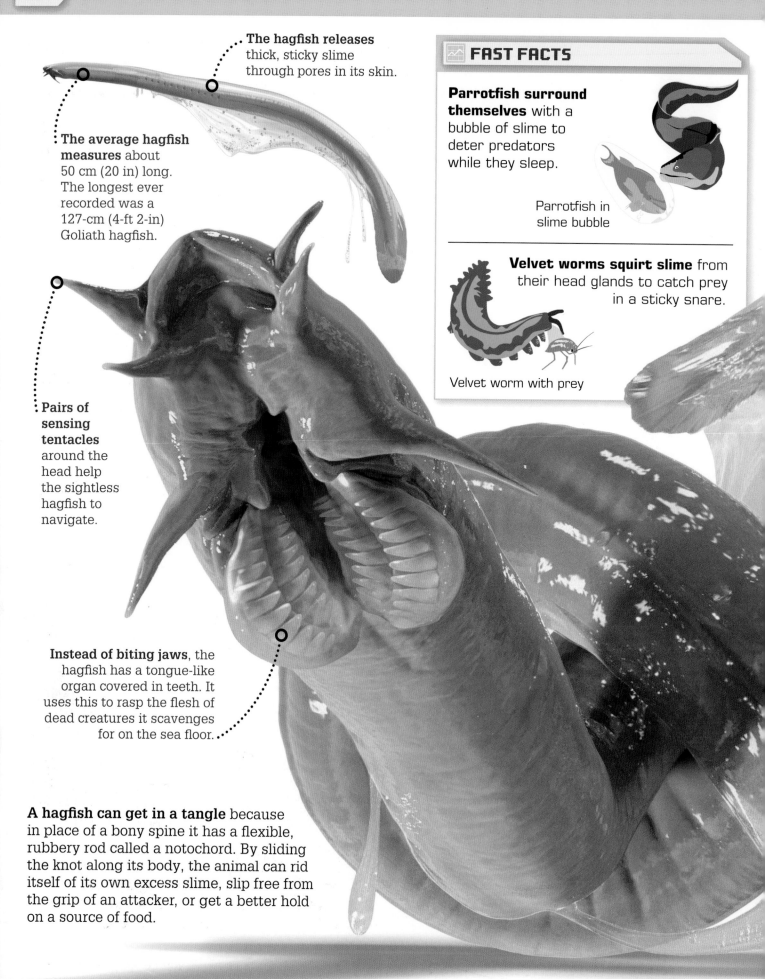

The hagfish releases thick, sticky slime through pores in its skin.

The average hagfish measures about 50 cm (20 in) long. The longest ever recorded was a 127-cm (4-ft 2-in) Goliath hagfish.

Pairs of sensing tentacles around the head help the sightless hagfish to navigate.

Instead of biting jaws, the hagfish has a tongue-like organ covered in teeth. It uses this to rasp the flesh of dead creatures it scavenges for on the sea floor.

FAST FACTS

Parrotfish surround themselves with a bubble of slime to deter predators while they sleep.

Parrotfish in slime bubble

Velvet worms squirt slime from their head glands to catch prey in a sticky snare.

Velvet worm with prey

A hagfish can get in a tangle because in place of a bony spine it has a flexible, rubbery rod called a notochord. By sliding the knot along its body, the animal can rid itself of its own excess slime, slip free from the grip of an attacker, or get a better hold on a source of food.

The **hagfish** begins to **tie a knot** at the tail, then **slides it** halfway up its body.

Which fish ties itself in knots?

Jawless, **spineless**, and oozing bucketfuls of **slime**, a **hagfish** may not sound appealing, but it has a very **special talent**. It can **tie** its **eel-like body** into a perfect **knot**.

The scaleless body is covered with loose skin through which the hagfish absorbs some nutrients.

SLIME SPILL

A highway in Oregon, USA, turned into a river of slime in 2017 when a truck carrying thousands of hagfish for export spilled its load. Several cars were snared in the sticky mess before a clean-up operation began.

Brilliantly blue animals

The **natural world** gleams and glimmers with a **kaleidoscope of colours**, but only a small number of creatures are **truly blue**.

Blue dragon
This dazzling creature is a type of sea slug. Its blue back blends into the azure waters of the Indian and Pacific oceans to escape the attention of flying predators such as pelicans, while its blue-grey front acts as camouflage against fish below.

Mandarinfish
At home in Pacific Ocean reefs, this fish produces a bright blue pigment in its skin to warn off predators. It is unique among animals with backbones in being able to produce blue pigment.

Hyacinth macaw
This South American bird flashes across the sky in a shimmering blaze of blue because only blue light is reflected off its feathers. The pigment of the feathers is actually black.

Blue morpho butterfly
This pretty South American butterfly has microscopic scales on top of its wings that reflect blue light, "flashing" in contrast with their brown undersides when in flight to make it appear and disappear.

Poison dart frog
Discovered in South America in 1968, the vivid blue poison dart frog has tiny crystals under its skin that catch the light and make it appear blue, acting as an alert to predators.

LONGEST FANGS

Africa's Gaboon viper has the longest fangs of any snake, at 5 cm (2 in). Just one bite delivers enough venom to kill a person.

Which is the longest snake?

Mighty Medusa, a **reticulated python**, holds the **world record** for the **longest snake** in captivity. She measures **7.67 m** (25 ft 2 in) long. Sightings of longer snakes have been reported in the wild.

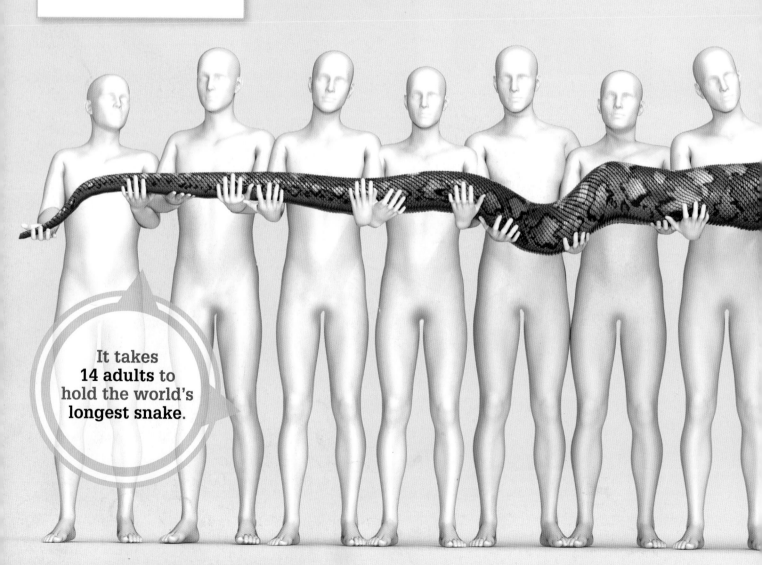

It takes **14 adults** to hold the world's **longest snake.**

📊 FAST FACTS

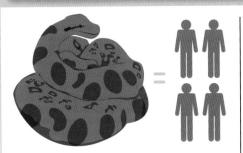

The world's heaviest snake is the green anaconda, weighing 227 kg (500 lb) — as much as four average adults.

The smallest snake is the Barbados threadsnake. At only 10 cm (4 in) long, it can fit onto a coin.

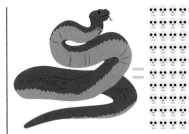

The snake with the deadliest venom is the inland taipan. A bite contains enough venom to kill 100 people.

Reticulated pythons are the longest snakes on Earth, growing to an average of 5 m (16 ft) long. When measured in 2011, Medusa weighed a whopping 158 kg (350 lb), thanks to a diet of rabbits, rodents, hogs, and deer.

The net-like pattern of the python's skin is known as "reticulated" and provides camouflage in dense forests.

The mouth can open wide but the python cannot chew, so animal prey must be swallowed whole.

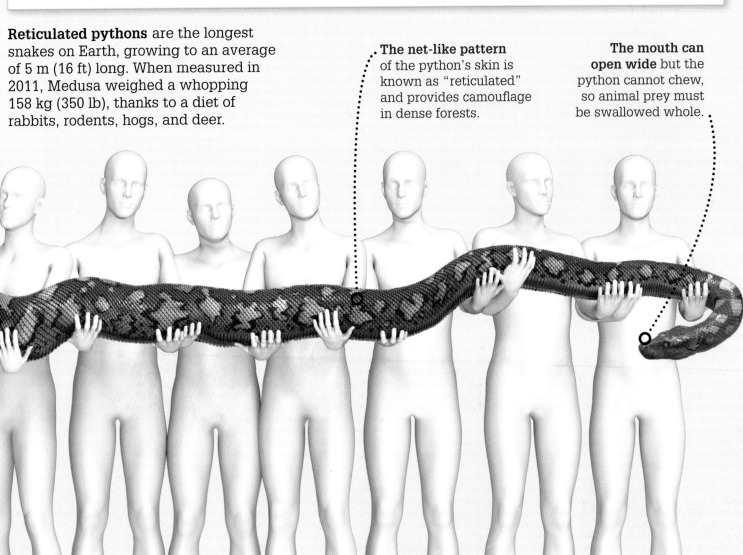

Kodiak bears are omnivorous brown bears that live on the Kodiak islands of Alaska, USA, where they mainly hunt salmon, but also eat berries, grass, and occasionally elk.

Bears are adapted to their environment, generally being bigger in cold regions because a large body size helps them to retain heat. This line-up shows estimated standing heights for the largest adult male of each species. Females are smaller.

Polar bears are bigger than most types of brown bear. Skilled hunters, they target seals to boost their body fat for warmth in the icy Arctic.

Spectacled bears, named for their facial fur pattern, survive life in the Andes Mountains of South America by eating plentiful plants.

The **Kodiak bear** stands about **twice the height** of an **average adult human**.

3 m
9 ft 11 in

2.5 m
8 ft 2 in

1 m
3 ft 3 in

0.5 m
1 ft 8 in

3.25 m
(10 ft 8 in)

3 m
(9 ft 11 in)

2 m
(6 ft 7 in)

How big is a bear?

Standing up to **3.25 m** (10 ft 8 in) **tall** and **weighing** as much as **680 kg** (1,500 lb), **Kodiak bears** – a type of brown bear native to Alaska – are the world's **biggest bears**.

Giant pandas from China eat bamboo shoots, using gripping paws, strong jaws, and flat teeth to tear, chew, and break down this tough plant.

Sun bears are the smallest of bears. They have long, sharp claws to rip into bees' nests in the rainforests of Southeast Asia.

1.9 m
(6 ft 3 in)

1.75 m
(5 ft 9 in)

1.4 m
(4 ft 7 in)

FAST FACTS

American and Asiatic black bears are separate species, but both are skilled tree climbers. American ones are the most common bear species, while Asiatic bears are vulnerable.

American black bear cub in tree

Sun bears have sticky tongues about 25 cm (10 in) long, which they use to extract termites, ants, and larvae from crevices, and honey from bees' nests — earning them the nickname "honey bears".

What animal vomits its stomach?

If we've eaten something bad, we can **regurgitate** the **contents** of our **stomach** to **get rid of it**. Some animals, such as horses or rats, cannot – but **frogs** can **vomit** their **entire stomach**.

A frog can **throw up** its **stomach** to eliminate toxic prey.

FAST FACTS

The world's smallest frog is *Paedophryne amauensis*. At just 7 mm (¼ in) long, it can sit on a US one-dime coin.

The frog can weigh more than 3 kg (7 lb) – about the same as a newborn baby.

The world's biggest frog is the Goliath frog, measuring up to 32 cm (12½ in) long – longer than a regulation rugby ball.

Frogs turn their stomachs inside out to get rid of poisons in a process called "gastric eversion". Once the toxins are removed, the frog swallows its stomach back inside its body, all in less than one second.

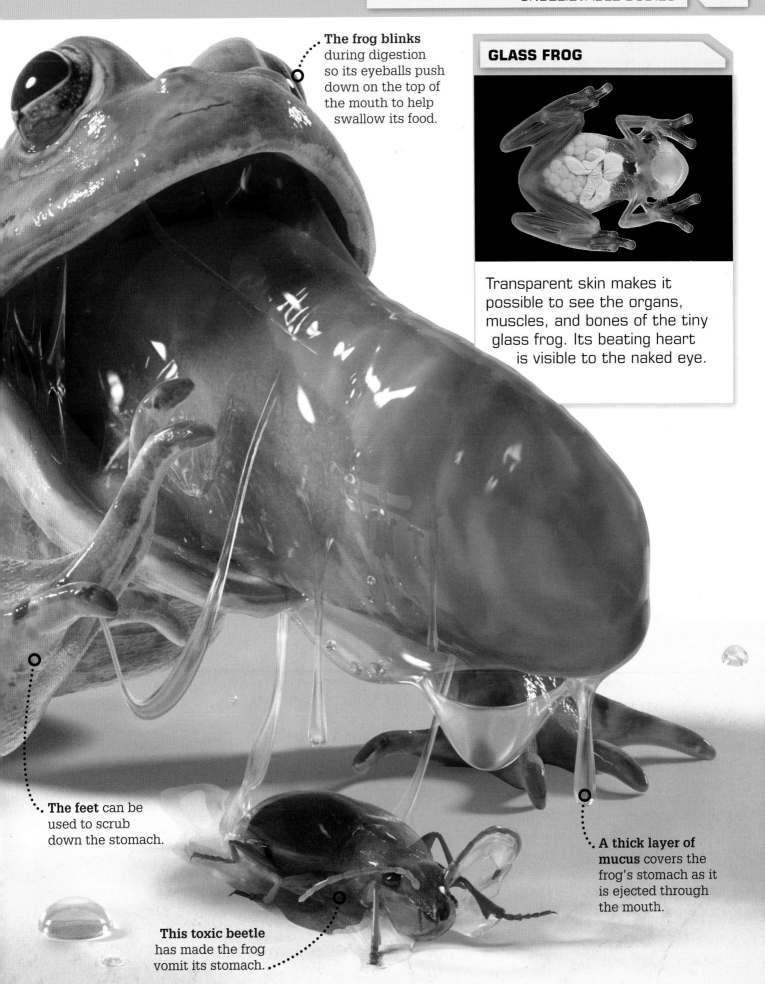

The frog blinks during digestion so its eyeballs push down on the top of the mouth to help swallow its food.

GLASS FROG

Transparent skin makes it possible to see the organs, muscles, and bones of the tiny glass frog. Its beating heart is visible to the naked eye.

The feet can be used to scrub down the stomach.

A thick layer of mucus covers the frog's stomach as it is ejected through the mouth.

This toxic beetle has made the frog vomit its stomach.

Which crab is the biggest?

On land, the **coconut crab** is the **world's largest** crab and biggest invertebrate. It also has the **most powerful grip** in the animal kingdom.

Colossal coconut crabs inhabit many islands in the Indian and Pacific oceans. The adult coconut crab only goes into the sea to lay eggs. Crab larvae hatch and stay underwater for 20–30 days before moving onto land.

The leg span of these gigantic crustaceans can be more than 1 m (3 ft), while their bodies may measure up to 40 cm (16 in) long.

A **coconut crab** can easily wrap its **giant legs** around a **basketball.**

Six strong, jointed legs help the crab to climb trees and harvest coconuts. A pair of tiny rear legs is concealed in the shell.

COCONUT CRACKER

As their name suggests, coconut crabs eat coconuts. Their huge pincers crack open the tough husks to reach the flesh inside.

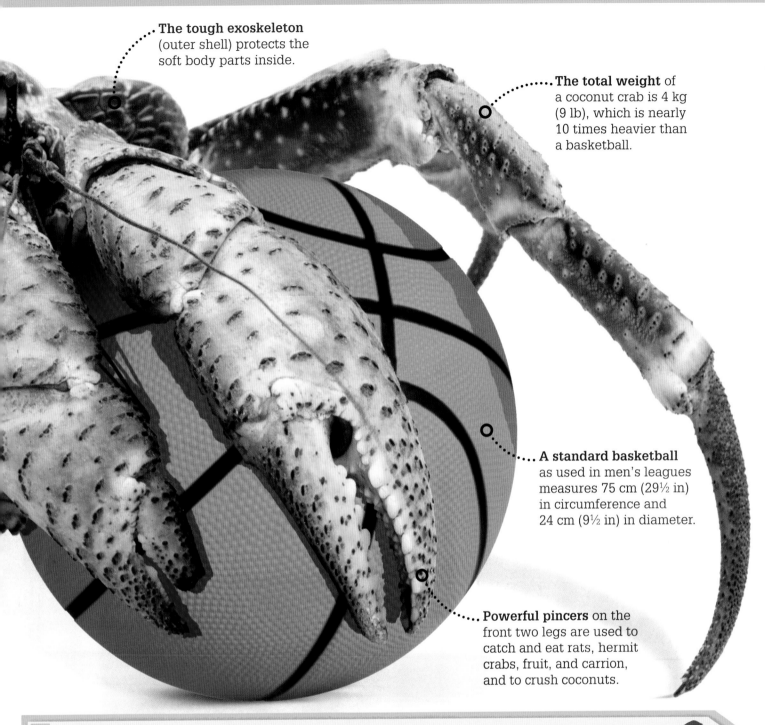

The tough exoskeleton (outer shell) protects the soft body parts inside.

The total weight of a coconut crab is 4 kg (9 lb), which is nearly 10 times heavier than a basketball.

A standard basketball as used in men's leagues measures 75 cm (29½ in) in circumference and 24 cm (9½ in) in diameter.

Powerful pincers on the front two legs are used to catch and eat rats, hermit crabs, fruit, and carrion, and to crush coconuts.

📈 FAST FACTS

The Japanese giant spider crab is the largest sea-dwelling crab, weighing 18 kg (40 lb). Its leg span is 4 m (13 ft) — as wide as a car is long.

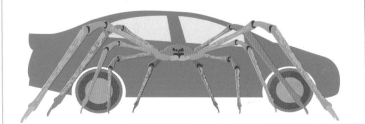

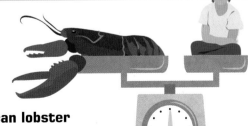

The American lobster is the world's heaviest crustacean, weighing up to 20 kg (44 lb) — as much as a six-year-old.

Costumed crabs

These **creative crustaceans** use natural accessories and even other creatures as brilliant **disguises** to go unnoticed or **deter predators**.

Orangutan crab
This small, tropical crab has a vibrant colour and fine hair similar to that of an orangutan. The crab sometimes collects stony fragments, bits of seaweed, and broken shells to cover its hairy legs.

Spider decorator crab
Using its long legs, this crab pulls living algae and sponges onto its body. Any sea life added to the mix that can't move away continues to grow on the crab, resulting in a complete camouflage.

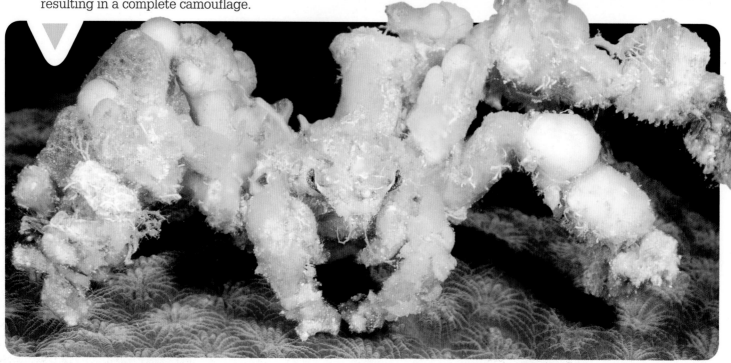

Boxer crab
This crab packs a punch by grabbing small sea anemones in its front claws to use in self-defence. The frilly anemones earn this species its alternative name, the pom-pom crab.

Sea urchin crab
The urchin crab is always dressed to kill. This species carries a sea urchin on its back like a spiky shield to ward off predators. The crab has strong back limbs to support this weighty addition.

···· **Mushroom anemone**

Decorator crab
With hooked hairs to attach anemones, algae, coral, and seaweed all over its body, this crab is a real fashion leader. As these natural accessories continue to grow, the disguise becomes more elaborate.

PUTTING OFF PREDATORS

An Asian geometrid moth at rest protects itself with an extraordinary piece of mimicry. The pattern on the moth's spread wings looks just like two flies feeding on a bird dropping, which may well repel would-be predators. To make its disguise doubly convincing, the moth even gives off the smell of droppings.

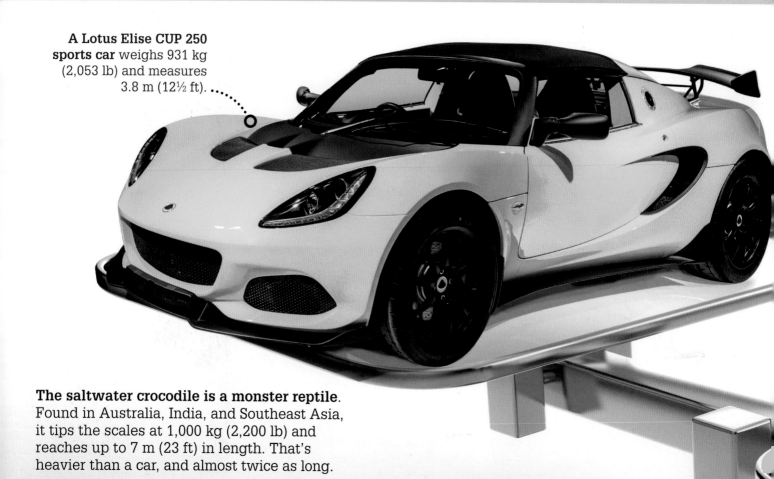

A Lotus Elise CUP 250 sports car weighs 931 kg (2,053 lb) and measures 3.8 m (12½ ft).

The saltwater crocodile is a monster reptile. Found in Australia, India, and Southeast Asia, it tips the scales at 1,000 kg (2,200 lb) and reaches up to 7 m (23 ft) in length. That's heavier than a car, and almost twice as long.

Which reptile is the heaviest?

The **saltwater crocodile** is a **record-breaking** reptile, taking first prize as the **heaviest reptile** on Earth. This colossal crocodile can weigh up to a staggering **1,000 kg** (2,200 lb).

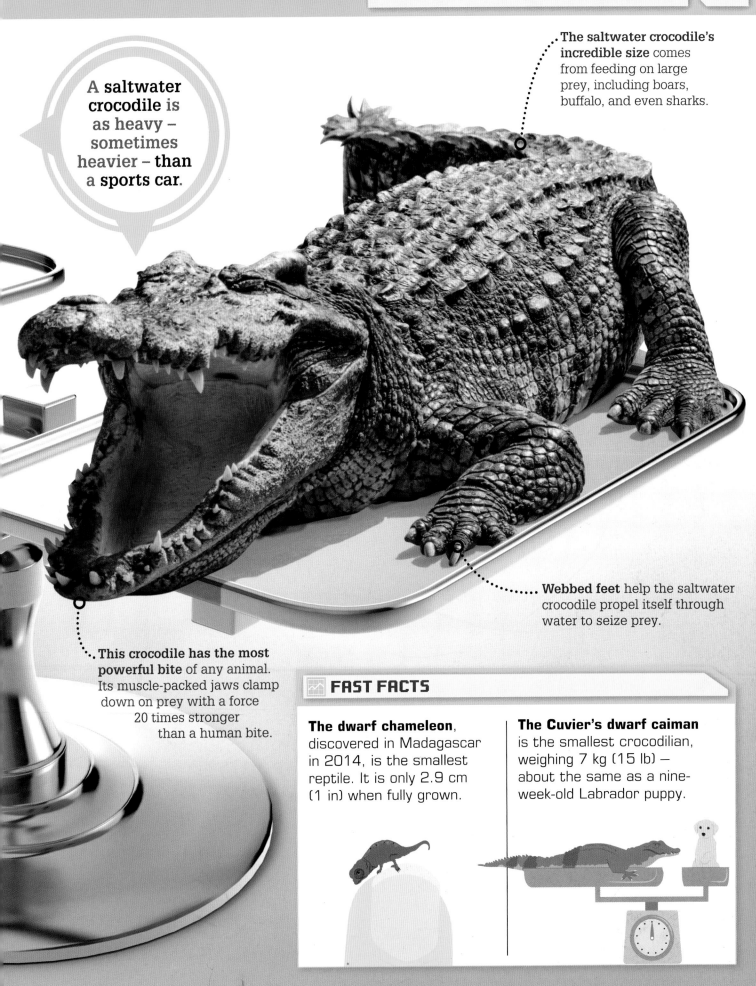

A **saltwater crocodile** is as heavy – sometimes heavier – **than a sports car**.

The saltwater crocodile's incredible size comes from feeding on large prey, including boars, buffalo, and even sharks.

Webbed feet help the saltwater crocodile propel itself through water to seize prey.

This crocodile has the most powerful bite of any animal. Its muscle-packed jaws clamp down on prey with a force 20 times stronger than a human bite.

📈 FAST FACTS

The dwarf chameleon, discovered in Madagascar in 2014, is the smallest reptile. It is only 2.9 cm (1 in) when fully grown.

The Cuvier's dwarf caiman is the smallest crocodilian, weighing 7 kg (15 lb) — about the same as a nine-week-old Labrador puppy.

3,000 teeth

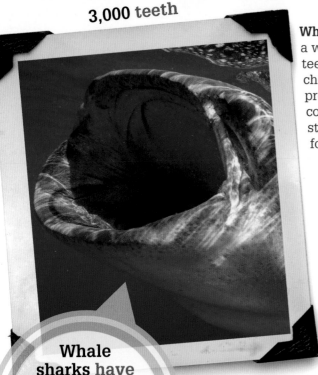

Whale sharks have a whopping 3,000 teeth, but not for chewing large prey. Its mouth contains filters for straining plankton food from the water.

Whale sharks have 300 rows of tiny teeth in their 1.5-m (5-ft) wide mouths.

100 teeth

A giant armadillo has about 100 teeth, which is more than any other land mammal.

Who has the most teeth?

From big biters to giant gnashers, here are the champion chewers and chompers. The **whale shark** has **3,000 tiny teeth** in total, while the great white shark can grow **30,000 teeth in its lifetime**.

The great white shark is top of the ocean food chain. It has mighty jaws and 300 sharp, triangular teeth in up to seven rows to bite into prey. Teeth are shed and replaced continuously, with new teeth moving up from behind.

32 teeth

Animals use their teeth to eat food. Different tooth shapes reveal their varied diets: carnivores have sharp canine teeth to tear into meat, while herbivores have flat, ridged, grinding teeth to chew tough plants.

A child grows 20 "milk", or baby, teeth by the time she is three. These gradually fall out and are replaced with 32 new teeth by adulthood.

A male narwhal has one canine tooth, which can grow 3 m (10 ft) long. It can be seen when the whale surfaces above the Arctic waters.

One tooth

14 teeth

300 teeth

A male Asian elephant has up to 14 teeth at one time. The two ivory tusks are the largest and the rest, inside the mouth, are used to chew on tough vegetation.

A leaf-tailed gecko has more than 300 teeth, used to grab hold of insect prey on the island of Madagascar.

Swimming with **rays**

With a wingspan up to 9 m (29 ft), the giant oceanic manta ray is the world's largest ray. These gentle giants glide through tropical, subtropical, and warm temperate waters all around the world. Among the cleverest creatures on Earth, they have the largest brain of any fish and can even recognize their own reflection in a mirror.

Giant manta rays have long been hunted for their gill plates, which are used in Chinese medicine, and their sheer size means that they are easily caught in fishing nets. This has reduced the global population of giant rays by one third in just three generations, making the species vulnerable to extinction.

Giant manta rays give **birth** to **one pup every two to three years** and may **live** for up to **40 years.**

However, ecotourism is changing attitudes, aided by what conservationists call "manta-nomics". In Peru, fishermen know the rays are now worth more alive than dead. Rather than fishing, they take tourists out on their boats to observe and swim with the rays. Moreover, it is illegal today in many places to capture, sell, or eat the rare giant manta ray.

BACK · FROM · THE · BRINK

CONSERVATION

Naturally curious
Each ray displays its own personality, but they share a curiosity and love of swimming alongside deep-sea divers.

Bald animals

We expect **mammals** to look **furry**, and most of them do. Among the exceptions with **bald** or nearly bald skin are, of course, humans. Some **hairless** animals, such as certain breeds of **cats and dogs**, or even **guinea pigs**, are popular pets.

Bald uakari
The bare, bright-red face of this bald-headed South American monkey shows that the animal is healthy. If it was sickly, it would look much paler. The bald uakari lives in the treetops of Amazonian rainforests.

Sphynx cat
The first sphynx kittens were born by chance to cats with normal fur, but now they are specially bred. Sphynxes have fine, soft fuzz on their bodies, but no whiskers.

Skinny pig
Among the newest crazes for bald pets is the hairless guinea pig, known as a skinny pig. It comes in various colours and has just a few fluffy patches of hair on its nose and feet.

Naked mole rat
This little pink rodent from East Africa lives in underground colonies. It has almost bare skin, tiny ears, and very poor sight. Well suited to its dark, warm tunnels, this animal may survive for 30 years.

Peruvian Inca Orchid
For hundreds of years, this hairless dog with the flowery name was known only in Peru. It is now famous worldwide as a pet and show dog. Some puppies are born with normal coats.

What bird has the biggest bill?

The **Australian pelican** has a record-breaking **bill**, measuring up to **50 cm** (20 in) **long**. It uses the bill like a giant fishing net to **scoop up** water and prey.

A hook at the end of the upper bill and the bill's jagged edge help the bird to grip slippery fish.

This Australian water bird uses its sensitive bill to detect crustaceans, fish, and even turtles to eat. Pelicans catch this prey with water in an expandable throat pouch, then drain the water out and jerk their head back to swallow the meal whole.

The throat pouch is attached to the lower bill. It scoops up water to catch prey. When the pelican swallows, it uses its tongue muscles to expel the water.

1 litre
1 litre
1 litre
1 litre

A pelican's bill can hold **13 litres** (3 gallons) of **water**.

Wings with black feathered edges can have a span of up to 2.5 m (8 ft 2 in), making the pelican one of the largest flying birds. It can weigh up to 6.8 kg (15 lbs).

📊 **FAST FACTS**

The kiwi is the only bird with nostrils at the tip of its beak. Kiwis have an acute sense of smell for sniffing out insects and worms in the soil.

North Island brown kiwi

The sword-billed hummingbird has the longest bill in relation to body length. Measuring 10 cm (4 in), the bill is longer than the body.

What's got the biggest horns?

A **Texas longhorn**, called Poncho Via, has the **world's biggest horns**. Living on a farm in Alabama, USA, this steer's horns stretch **3.2 m** (10 ft 5 in) from tip to tip.

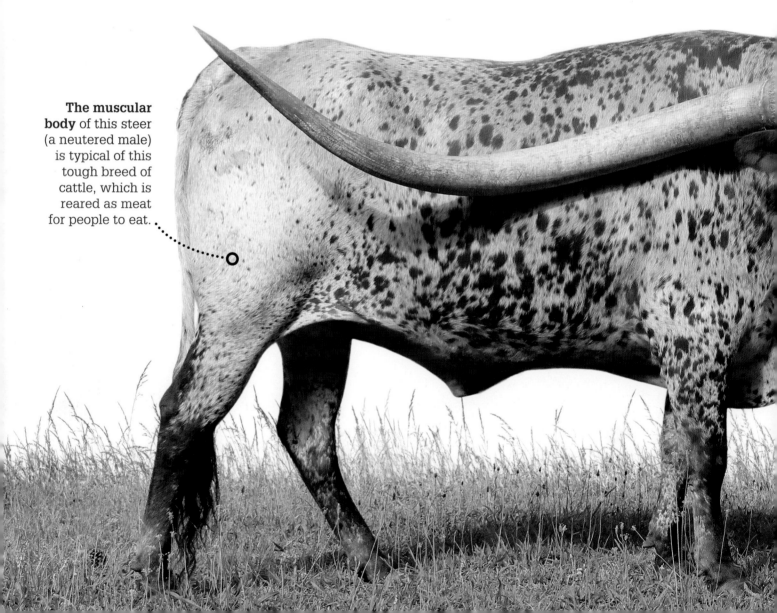

The muscular body of this steer (a neutered male) is typical of this tough breed of cattle, which is reared as meat for people to eat.

Most Texas longhorns have horns that curve straight up – however, Poncho Via's are a curious exception. While horns found in cows, sheep, goats, and antelope are permanent structures, antlers grow seasonally. Antlers, which deer have, fall off and are replaced each year.

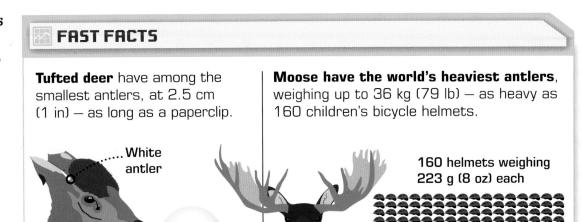

FAST FACTS

Tufted deer have among the smallest antlers, at 2.5 cm (1 in) – as long as a paperclip.

White antler

Moose have the world's heaviest antlers, weighing up to 36 kg (79 lb) – as heavy as 160 children's bicycle helmets.

160 helmets weighing 223 g (8 oz) each

=

The average arm span of an adult male is 1.8 m (5 ft 10 in).

This farm animal's exceptionally long horns are purely for display. Horned wild animals, however, use their horns as a weapon in fights for territory and mates.

Horns are made of bone and keratin, which is the same substance that makes hair and fingernails.

Poncho Via's horns are **twice the length of a man's outstretched arms.**

HORNED REPTILE

Scaly horns extend above the eyes of Africa's horned viper. They work as a pair of shields, protecting this desert snake's eyes against scratchy sand.

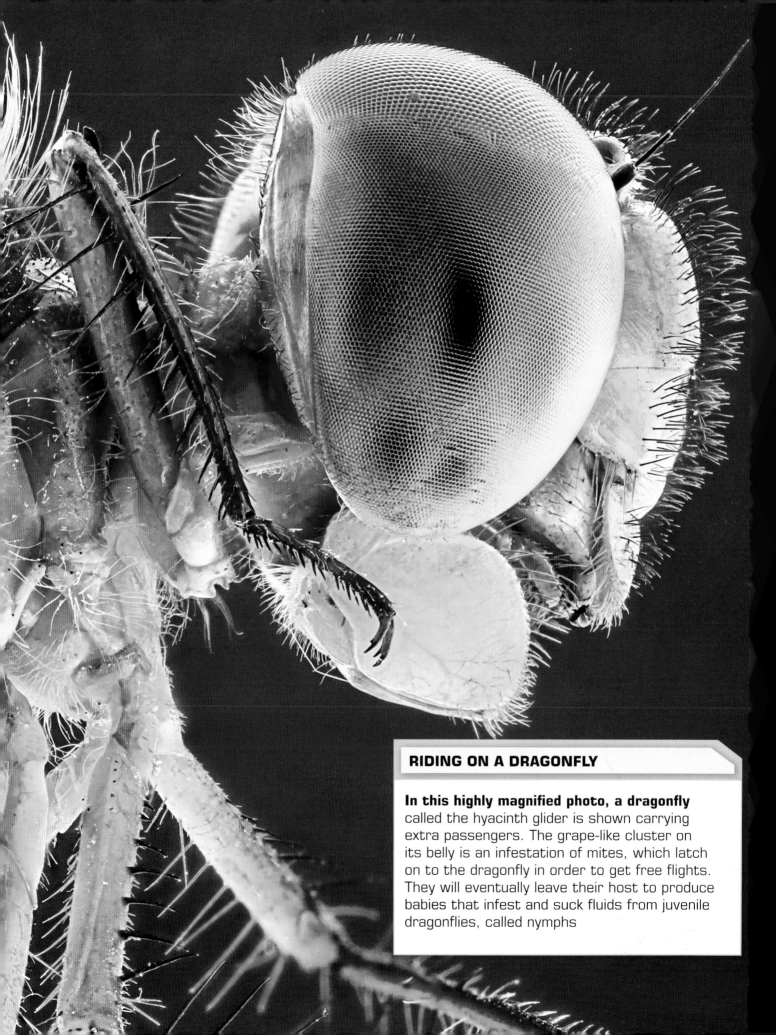

RIDING ON A DRAGONFLY

In this highly magnified photo, a dragonfly called the hyacinth glider is shown carrying extra passengers. The grape-like cluster on its belly is an infestation of mites, which latch on to the dragonfly in order to get free flights. They will eventually leave their host to produce babies that infest and suck fluids from juvenile dragonflies, called nymphs

The long snout is 40 times more sensitive than a human's nose, enabling the anteater to sniff out prey over long distances.

Sharp claws are used to tear open ant and termite hills without destroying them for future meals.

The anteater's tongue is as long as 15 scoops of ice cream.

The tongue is covered with sharp spines and coated in sticky saliva to lap up insects.

An anteater's toothless jaws contain a very long tongue, measuring one third of its body length. After lapping up ants, the anteater uses the strong muscles of its tongue, which is attached to a pad on its breastbone, to pull the tongue in again.

What animal has the longest tongue?

The giant anteater has the longest lick of any land animal. Its tongue extends 61 cm (2 ft) and flicks 160 times a minute to catch 30,000 ants or termites a day.

Termite

FAST FACTS

The rosette-nosed pygmy chameleon has the longest tongue of any animal relative to its body size. With a tongue that accelerates faster than a sports car, this lizard can snare prey in just 0.02 seconds.

2.5 times body length

The tube-lipped nectar bat has the longest tongue of any mammal relative to its body size. Its tongue has tiny hairs to pick up nectar from the long, tubular flowers on which it feeds.

1.5 times body length

Unbelievable bodies facts

ANIMALS WITH THE LONGEST CLAWS

The **giant armadillos** and **anteaters** of South America have the **longest claws of any animal**, which they use to **rip open termite mounds** in search of food. Their **long claws** are also used in **self-defence** against **jaguars**.

The cassowary's claws can injure cats and dogs.

A sloth's claws help it to grip branches.

Giant armadillo
20 cm (8 in)

Giant anteater
18 cm (7 in)

Southern cassowary
12.5 cm (5 in)

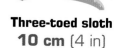

Three-toed sloth
10 cm (4 in)

LONGEST NECKS

• A **giraffe** is the tallest land mammal. Its **neck** can be up to **2.5 m** (8 ft 2 in) **long**, almost half of the giraffe's height. It has only **seven neck bones**.

• An **ostrich's neck** can be up to **1 m** (3 ft 3 in) **long**, which is about half of the bird's height. The **neck** has **19 bones** and can turn **180 degrees**.

• A **giraffe weevil** has the **longest neck** of any **insect** relative to body size. Its neck makes up two-thirds of its **2 cm** ($^7/_8$ in) length.

AMAZING ANTLERS

Caribou have the **largest antlers relative to body size**. The **antlers** weigh up to **16 kg** (35 lb) and grow **1.5 m** (4 ft 11 in) long. They roam North America, Europe, Asia, and Greenland.

1.5 m (4 ft 1 in)

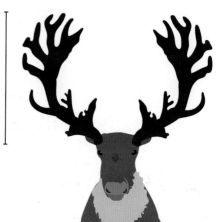

SPIKY ANIMALS

◄ Lionfish

These fish grow up to **47 cm** ($18^{1}/_{2}$ in) long. Their **spines**, which can reach up to **9 cm** ($3^{1}/_{2}$ in) in length, deliver toxic venom to prey through puncture wounds.

► Sea urchin

The body of a sea urchin can be up to **10 cm** (4 in) across, but its spines grow as long as **20 cm** (8 in).

◄ Porcupine

Some porcupines can grow up to **90 cm** (35 in) long, while the longest quills reach **51 cm** (20 in) in length – more than half the length of the animal.

LOTS OF **LEGS**

A **centipede** has hundreds of legs, and none more so than *Himantarium gabrielis*, with up to **354 legs**. Found in the Mediterranean, this species grows up to **22 cm** ($9^{1}/_{2}$ in) **in length**. All centipedes have **two legs per body segment**.

The **millipede** species *Illacme plenipes* has up to **192 segments** with a total of **768 legs**. Found in California, USA, it grows up to **3 cm** ($1^{1}/_{4}$ in) **long**. All millipedes have **four legs per body segment**.

TOXIC TERRORS

• A **marine cone snail** delivers a **cocktail of toxins** that can paralyse fish. It is estimated that one snail has enough venom to **kill 700 people**.

• The **blue-ringed octopus** can injure or even kill a person with **just one bite**. Its venom is 1,000 times more powerful than cyanide, and has enough venom in its saliva to **kill 26 people**.

• A **golden poison frog** secretes enough poison through its toxic skin to **kill 10 people**. It gets the poison from invertebrates it eats. Its **only predator is a snake** that is resistant to the poison.

• The **Australian box jellyfish** has one of the **most deadly venoms** in the world. It contains toxins that attack the heart, nervous system, and skin – causing blisters on contact, if not **death**.

MONSTER MOUTH

The bowhead whale has the largest mouth in the animal kingdom, measuring up to **6 m** (20 ft) wide – more than the length of three people.

Strength and speed

From super-swimmers to territory defenders, many animals can out-perform humans with their astonishing strength and speed. Discover the unexpected animals from around the world that achieve stunning feats of physical power and endurance.

Dung beetles prove that some of the smallest animals are also the strongest. The male dung beetle can move dungballs that weigh up to 1,141 times its own body weight. Their 3-cm (1¼-in) bodies are packed with muscles that enable them to lift these extraordinary weights.

Which **bird** flies **higher** than an **aeroplane?**

Birds fly high on long migrations or to help them spot food. The **highest bird flight** ever recorded was by a **Rüppell's vulture**, which soared above the altitude of an aeroplane.

Aeroplane altitude
10,668 m (35,000 ft)

The standard cruising altitude of a passenger plane is 10,668 m (35,000 ft), although they can fly higher or lower.

The **Rüppell's vulture** can fly **600 m (2,000 ft)** higher than a passenger plane.

This giant wingspan measures up to 2.4 m (7 ft 10 in). Only slow beating of the wings or strong winds are needed to stay airborne.

In 1973, a Rüppell's vulture flying over its African homeland collided with a passenger jet. Collisions like this are rare and the vulture usually flies at a lower altitude. This bird may have reached this great height when gliding on thermal winds.

The Rüppell's vulture can reach a top speed of 35 km/h (22 mph) and flies for up to seven hours a day.

Vulture altitude
11,280 m (37,000 ft)

PROTECTIVE POSE

Although the Rüppell's vulture is a high-flyer, it swoops down to the ground to scavenge carrion. To protect its food the vulture adopts an aggressive stance by lifting its wings and standing tall.

FAST FACTS

Some birds can reach incredible heights, making the world's tallest landmarks look tiny.

Rüppell's vulture
11,280 m (37,000 ft)

Boeing 737
10,668 m (35,000 ft)

Common crane
10,058 m (33,000 ft)

Mount Everest (tallest mountain)
8,848 m (29,029 ft)

Bar-headed goose
8,534 m
(28,000 ft)

Average skydive
up to 4,000 m
(13,000 ft)

Burj Khalifa
(tallest building)
830 m (2,723 ft)

Creature combat

Many animals face a **fight for survival**. Within their **own species**, they **spar** to win the affections of a **mate**, prove **dominance**, or **take over territory**.

Hippopotamus
Aggressive by nature, hippopotamuses come well-equipped for conflict, with large tusks and gaping jaws. These African giants battle each other to establish dominance within a group, the winner often causing the other serious injury.

Red kangaroo
These Australian marsupials are ever ready to deal a knock-out blow. Dominant males grapple and kick with their powerful legs and sharp claws, scrapping over potential mates.

Komodo dragon
Reptiles can turn rivals during mating season. On Komodo Island, Indonesia, male dragons fight for a female by hissing loudly before wrestling together. The winner is decided when one is overpowered by the strength of the other.

Grey heron
Brawling birds unleash mid-air mayhem in disputes over territory. These two grey herons face each other head-on, filling the skies with flapping wings and flying feathers. This predatory bird found in Europe, Asia, and Africa may even use its beak to grasp an opponent by the neck.

Giraffe
The world's tallest animal is not built for battle, but dominant giraffe bulls (males) on the African savannah still skirmish over mates. They lash out with their legs and thrash with their necks to topple the other and triumph.

A GOOD CATCH

Anchored to waterside plants, a raft spider hauls up its lunch. Fishing spiders such as this one hunt in fresh water all over the world, and some are able to lift prey many times their size. This striped spider, found in Europe, uses floating vegetation as a raft from which to seize fish. It can also swim, dive, and even run on water.

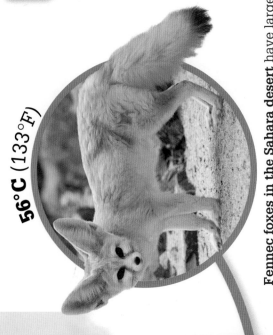

56°C (133°F)

Fennec foxes in the Sahara desert have large ears that give off heat and keep them cool. They escape the most scorching daytime heat by hiding underground and hunting at night.

42°C (108°F)

The Pompeii worm is only 5 cm (2 in) long but lives tail-first in the fiery heat of volcanic ocean vents. They live in large colonies and are armed with thermal "blankets" to survive the heat.

Most humans can only live comfortably within a temperature range of 4.44°C (40°F) to 35°C (95°F).

50°C (122°F)
40°C (104°F)
30°C (86°F)
20°C (68°F)
10°C (50°F)
0°C (32°F)

What animals are survival experts?

From desert foxes to polar penguins, some creatures live in extreme places. These animals have amazing adaptations to beat the heat and fight the freeze.

The wood frog is an astonishing amphibian that produces chemicals enabling it to freeze alive during icy Alaskan winters. Both its heart and breathing stops for weeks before it defrosts in time for summer.

-1°C (30°F)

-2°C (28°F)

Icefish in the freezing cold Southern Ocean create their own natural antifreeze to stop ice crystals forming in their bloodstream.

-101°C (-150°F)

The tiny red flat bark beetle copes with the bone-chilling temperatures of the North American Arctic by deliberately dehydrating before producing antifreeze crystals.

-20°C
(-4°F)

-40°C
(-40°F)

-60°C
(-76°F)

-80°C
(-112°F)

-100°C
(-148°F)

-200°C
(-328°F)

Absolute zero

-40°C (-40°F)

Depending on the extreme conditions, animals cope in different ways. Desert animals often live in underground shelters or burrows and adopt a nocturnal lifestyle to escape the heat. On the other hand, creatures living in the cold may have fatter, furrier bodies or special adaptations to stop their blood freezing.

Antarctica's emperor penguins rely on their feathers and body fat to withstand plummeting temperatures and battering winds of up to 145 km/h (90 mph).

Tardigrades survive extreme hot and cold conditions that would kill other creatures.

-273°C (-459°F)

Tiny tardigrades are just 1 mm (0.04 in) long, but they can cope with the most extreme conditions on Earth. They can survive in boiling water up to 148°C (300°F) or in ice, and live without water for a decade.

What animal is the **fastest swimmer?**

Olympic swimmers look slow when compared with **streamlined sharks** and **fast-moving fish**. But everything gets overtaken by the **sailfish**, which tops **109 km/h** (68 mph).

The top speeds of the ocean's fastest movers can easily splash past those of the fastest human. If all kinds of marine life came together for a race in a standard 50-m (164-ft) Olympic swimming pool, our best athletes would lag far behind.

Orca
56 km/h (35 mph)

This graceful penguin propels itself through the water about three times faster than any other penguin species.

Gentoo penguin
35 km/h (22 mph)

These turbo-charged turtles are the world's fastest reptiles, with the stamina to swim for up to five hours.

Olympic champion Florent Manaudou, from France, set a new record when he swam the 50-m (164-ft) freestyle race in 20.26 seconds in 2014.

Human
9 km/h (6 mph)

Leatherback turtle
35 km/h (22 mph)

This super-speedy fish uses its streamlined sail-like dorsal fin and fast-flicking tail to hit lightning speeds.

Sailfish
109 km/h (68 mph)

1.64 seconds

The time it would take the sailfish to swim 50 m (164 ft), with its competitors below.

The speediest shark is a heavyweight predator that can leap clean out of the water to catch prey.

Shortfin mako shark
74 km/h (45 mph)

2.49 seconds

The **sailfish is the fastest in water** and 11 times faster than an Olympic swimmer.

3.24 seconds

These mighty marine mammals use their supreme size, shape, and strength to speed through the open ocean.

They may be bulky and blubbery on land, but these sea lions are athletic and agile in water.

4.47 seconds

California sea lion
40 km/h (25 mph)

The common octopus uses jet propulsion to swim by sucking in and filtering out water to generate immense speed.

4.47 seconds

Common octopus
40 km/h (25 mph)

5.08 seconds

FLOATING FELINE

Unlike most big cats, tigers are skilled swimmers and confident in water. Their partially webbed paws and incredible strength enable them to hunt in rivers over distances of 6 km (4 miles). They also enjoy taking a dip to cool off on a warm day.

5.10 seconds

20.26 seconds

What animal is the **best hunter?**

Look to the skies for the **most successful predator** on Earth. The **dragonfly** is among the world's **best hunters** and **three times** more likely than **big cats** to catch its prey.

Animals adopt different tactics to catch their prey, with varying success. The top three hunters on land and in the air might surprise you. Some animals, including wild dogs, work as a team while others, such as cheetahs, give chase at high speeds. But dragonflies, with their super-quick reactions and huge eyes, are on the winner's podium.

Lionesses hunt in a team to ambush their grassland prey, but they are successful only 30 per cent of the time.

African wild dogs are skilled hunters and the second most successful. They work in packs of 20 to take down large animals like wildebeest, catching prey around 67 per cent of the time.

FAST FACTS

The harbour porpoise is one of the most successful underwater creatures, hunting fish with a success rate of around 90 per cent.

Rabbit

The golden eagle is a supreme hunter, but grabbing prey from the air is tough, so only 20 per cent of hunts end in success.

The komodo dragon is a patient hunter. This 3-m (10-ft) long lizard has a toxic bite that takes days to kill prey before it sniffs out the body to eat.

Dragonflies are fast fliers, moving in on prey at top speeds of 54 km/h (34 mph).

Cheetahs are daytime hunters, using sharp vision, camouflaged fur, and exceptional speed to take down antelope and zebras.

The dragonfly is the ultimate hunter. This insect's large eyes, muscle-packed wings, and super-fast reactions combine to help it catch mosquitoes on almost every attempt.

Dragonflies are top hunters and catch their prey with a 95 per cent success rate.

The cheetah is the world's fastest land animal, reaching speeds of up to 93 km/h (58 mph). Despite its speed, it takes third place on the podium as it catches its prey only 50 per cent of the time.

On the hunt
A Mauritius kestrel hovers in mid-air while using its sharp sight to scour the ground for prey.

Soaring
kestrel

Native to the island of Mauritius in the Indian Ocean, the Mauritius kestrel is one of the finest fliers around. Its body is entirely adapted for forest habitats, with short, rounded wings that enable smooth navigation through the dense woodland. This agility in the air allows the kestrel to hunt geckos, bugs, and smaller birds during short spurts of flight.

BACK · FROM · THE · BRINK

CONSERVATION

From **only four birds,** there are now an estimated **400 kestrels flying free** in Mauritius.

However, the Mauritius kestrel was once the world's rarest bird. In 1974, there were only four of them left in the wild, as the combined forces of deforestation and pesticides used in farming pushed this beautiful bird of prey to the brink of extinction.

Conservation groups took immediate action, breeding the surviving kestrels in captivity for later release. Between 1988 and 1991, captive breeding by the Peregrine Fund led to 46 kestrels being released into the wild.

During this time additional measures were introduced, including the use of nest boxes, assistance with feeding, and controls set on exotic predators. This has resulted in kestrel numbers rising into the hundreds, with around 100 breeding pairs in the wild today.

The ant's **strong mandibles** (jaws) grip the bee's antenna tightly in an amazing display of strength.

How strong is an ant?

Ants are incredibly strong for their size. The **strongest** ants can carry up to **5,000 times** their own weight, **more than any other animal.**

SUPER WEIGHTLIFTER

The Allegheny mound ant could be the strongest ant in the world. In test conditions, the ant's strong neck can bear weights 5,000 times its body weight.

A weaver ant can carry a bee 175 times heavier than its own body weight.

This weaver ant was spotted on a tree branch in Indonesia, carrying a dead bee to its nest. These 8-mm (⅓-in) long ants generally prey on small insects and honeydew – a sweet liquid produced by some bugs.

Insects such as bees are tempting prey for a weaver ant, who can feed on live insects or scavenge dead ones.

FAST FACTS

An elephant can lift up to 300 kg (660 lb) with its trunk alone. Elephants are strong enough to easily lift logs and even people.

In 1924, a pair of shire horses pulled an estimated 45,700 kg (100,750 lb), the weight of nine elephants!

PIRATE PREY

Above the prairie of San Juan Island National Park, USA, a young fox is caught in a mid-air tussle when a bald eagle swoops on the freshly caught rabbit held in its jaws. The persistent fox is lifted into the air before releasing the rabbit, leaving the eagle to fly off with its stolen prey. Eagles frequently steal prey from other hunters, in an act known as kleptoparasitism or piracy.

What animal moves the slowest?

Some species take life **slow and steady**, never crossing the finish line first. Slugs have among the **slowest motion** ever recorded on land, managing a sluggish **10 cm** (4 in) **per minute**.

The **banana slug** is 45 times slower than the **Galápagos tortoise**.

The **Galápagos tortoise** is one of the slowest reptiles, travelling only 4.5 m (15 ft) a minute. Its cumbersome shell hinders its progress.

SPORTY SNAILS

The World Snail Racing Championships are held annually in Norfolk, UK, with 200 competitors moving at a snail's pace. The first snail to reach the outer red circle wins a tankard of lettuce!

The sloth is the slowest-moving mammal, covering only 3.5 m (11½ ft) per minute on the ground. This is because sloths have a diet of leaves that provides them with very little energy.

Slugs such as the banana slug are among the slowest land animals, reaching speeds of 10 cm (4 in) a minute. But some microscopic creatures such as tardigrades may be even slower!

0.006 km/h
(0.004 mph)

0.05 km/h
(0.03 mph)

0.21 km/h
(0.13 mph)

The garden snail inches along at 83 cm (2½ ft) per minute because it has only one slimy foot.

0.27 km/h
(0.16 mph)

Animals move slowly for different reasons. Heavy, bulky creatures like tortoises move slowly because of their size and weight. Animals like snails lack joints, which limits their movement, while animals like sloths have low energy levels and tire quickly.

📊 FAST FACTS

Land animals can be slow but the sea is home to animals so slow they don't appear to move!

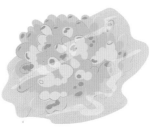

Sea sponges are the slowest animals, moving 1 mm (0.04 in) a day.

Sea stars use hundreds of tiny feet to travel 0.3 m (1 ft) a minute.

Dwarf seahorses, the slowest fish, swim 1.5 m (5 ft) an hour.

Greenland sharks move at only 1.2 km (¾ mile) an hour.

Strength and speed facts

SWIFTER THAN SWIFT

The **common swift** is one of the world's fastest birds, with speeds of up to **112 km/h** (70 mph). But the *Brazilian free-tailed bat* races ahead at **160 km/h** (100 mph).

Common swift · Brazilian free-tailed bat

SUPER SPEEDS

The fastest movers on Earth free-fall through the sky or race across land at **blistering speeds**, usually in pursuit of prey.

Pronghorn
100 km/h
(62 mph)

Cheetah
102 km/h (63 mph)

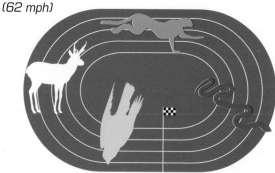

Peregrine falcon 389 km/h
(242 mph) in a free-fall dive

Black mamba
160 km/h
(100 mph)

BEST BREATH-HOLDERS

By holding their breath, some animals can stay underwater for long periods of time. The **Cuvier's beaked whale** is the mammal that can hold its breath the longest.

15 mins

Dolphins can hold their breath for up to **15 minutes**, by squeezing their blowhole shut.

27 mins

Emperor penguins go **27 minutes** without taking a breath when diving under water in search of fish.

40 mins

Sloths are surprisingly good swimmers and can hold their breath for up to **40 minutes**.

1 hr 30 mins

Sperm whales go up to **1 hour 30 minutes** without taking a breath.

2 hrs

American alligators manage to stay underwater for up to **2 hours** without coming up for air.

2 hrs

Elephant seals hold their breath for up to **2 hours**, diving up to 1,500 m (4,920 ft).

2 hrs 18 mins

Cuvier's beaked whales can hold their breath for up to **2 hours 18 minutes** during deep dives.

FASTEST FLYING INSECT

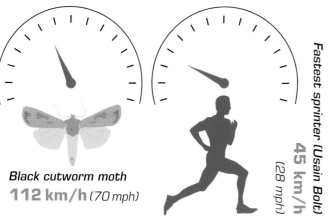

Black cutworm moth
112 km/h *(70 mph)*

Fastest sprinter (Usain Bolt)
45 km/h *(28 mph)*

BIGGEST KILLER

Spiders may be small and live on a diet of insects, but they kill more prey than any other animal — **eating** up to **800 million tonnes** of prey per year.

800m tonnes

FARTHEST MIGRATION

Animals migrate for **winter**, **food**, or **breeding** seasons but these three make the longest journeys.

• **Caribous** travel up to **4,404 km** (2,737 miles) per year in search of warmer weather during winter.
• **Northern elephant seals** swim **21,000 km** (13,049 miles) per year in the sea in pursuit of food.
• **Arctic terns** have the longest migration of any animal, travelling **71,000 km** (44,117 miles) per year.

Caribou   Northern elephant seal   Arctic tern

ELECTRIC shocker

These **cunning hunters** use high voltage electric shocks to **find**, **stun**, or **kill** prey. Many electricity sockets are 220 volts.

Electric eel
600 volts

Electric catfish
350 volts

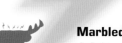

Marbled electric ray
220 volts

Stargazer 50 volts

LONGEST TAILS

▲ Long-tailed grass lizard
This slinky lizard has the **longest tail** relative to its **body length** of any reptile. These lizards grow up to **30 cm** (12 in) long, with the tail measuring up to **18 cm** (7 in).

▼ Long-eared jerboa This little rodent's body length is only **9 cm** (3¹/₂ in) at most, but the tail is **nearly twice** this length, at up to **16 cm** (6¹/₃ in).

▲ Red kangaroo
Male kangaroos' bodies grow up to **1.6 m** (5 ft 2 in) long with an extra **tail length** of **1.2 m** (3 ft 9 in).

Homes and hideaways

Many creatures need a safe place where they can shelter, sleep, or raise young. In the endless variety of the animal world, an ideal home could be a cave, a colony, a nest, or even another animal's discarded shell.

A hermit crab does not grow a shell of its own and has to protect its long, soft body using the empty shell of another creature. As the crab grows, it moves to a larger shell. Sometimes, crabs fight over the best shell to make their new home.

How big is an ant colony?

Leafcutter ants in Brazil built one of the **biggest insect colonies** ever found. Descending **8 m** (26 ft) **underground**, this sprawling subterranean shelter covered an area of **45 sq m** (500 sq ft).

Tunnels form a network of main routes and side routes connecting to chambers deep underground.

A colony that was once home to millions of leafcutter ants in Brazil was investigated in 2010 by insect experts. They filled the tunnels with 10 tonnes of concrete, let it set hard, then dug out the surrounding earth to reveal the incredible size of this ant kingdom.

Waste chambers around the edge of the colony are used to store waste material, including mould, dead ants, and harmful parasites.

This massive **ant colony** is the same size as a small **city apartment**.

BRAWNY BUGS

The leafcutter ant is a little powerhouse, capable of lifting 50 times its own body weight. This active, athletic species works very hard, collecting and carrying leaves for the colony on which the fungus food grows.

Entomologists study insects and their habitats to understand the part they play in the natural world.

Chambers containing fungus gardens are dotted around the ant colony. Eggs are laid inside here, then young larvae hatch from these eggs and feast on the fungus.

A large queen ant chooses the colony site, lays the eggs, and rules over millions of worker ants. She usually lives inside the largest fungus garden chamber.

6,400 m (21,000 ft)

The sleek, black Alpine chough is a member of the crow family. This bird flies easily in high mountain winds, and often builds its nests deep in holes or rock crevices.

6,000 m (19,680 ft)

6,000 m (19,680 ft)

Yaks are purpose-made for high altitudes, with huge, shaggy double coats. They also have splayed hooves for walking on snow, and exceptionally large hearts and lungs that help them get maximum oxygen from the air.

Few plants and animals can survive above 5,000 m (16,400 ft).

5,000 m (16,400 ft)

7,000 m (23,000 ft)

The intrepid **Himalayan jumping spider** has been found at 6,700 m (21,980 ft).

6,700 m (21,980 ft)

The Himalayan jumping spider lives at a higher altitude than any other animal. Found on some of the world's highest mountains – including the tallest, Mount Everest – this spider survives by feeding on insects that have been blown into its territory from lower slopes.

6,300 m (20,670 ft)

Springtails are tiny wingless insects that can survive year round in almost any conditions. The springtails found in the Himalayas are sometimes called "snow fleas".

Mountains are hostile habitats, with freezing cold conditions, rocky or icy terrain, and scarce food. However, the animals that live in such places are well equipped for survival, whether it is with thick fur, non-slip feet, or body systems that cope with low oxygen levels.

What animal lives at the highest altitude?

All kinds of animals live at high altitude, but the **Himalayan jumping spider** tops them all. There are many challenges living the high life, including freezing temperatures, extreme winds, and **limited oxygen**.

4,500 m (14,760 ft)

The **toad-headed lizard** can survive at higher altitudes than any other reptile. It is active during the day and shelters under stones and in cracks at night.

4,000 m (13,120 ft)

The world's highest permanently **inhabited town** is La Rinconada in the Peruvian Andes. More than 50,000 people have adjusted to life in the thin atmosphere of this gold-mining settlement.

5,100 m (16,730 ft)

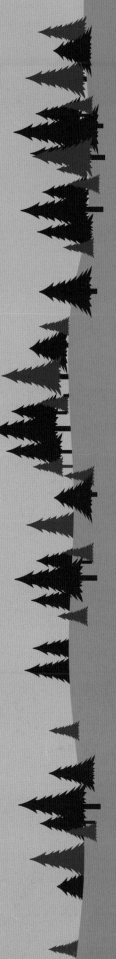

Are birds the only nest builders?

Birds rule the roost when it comes to **crafting nests**, but many other creatures build nests in **trees** or on the **ground**.

A colony of weaver ants sew leaves together with silk made by their young. This teamwork results in vast networks of football-sized nests in trees.

One **nest** can contain a **colony** of more than **500,000** weaver ants.

A nest provides a secure shelter for birds to raise their chicks. Some mammals, reptiles, and insects also build structures for their eggs and young, to host large colonies, or for sleeping in.

Chimpanzees build new nests in trees every evening for a good night's sleep. They knot branches together tightly to prevent any falls and layer leaves for pillows.

BRANCHING OUT

White terns are unusual birds because a female lays an egg directly on a branch instead of building a nest. When hatched, the chick steadies itself on the branch with its extremely strong claws.

A pregnant alligator prepares for her new hatchlings by constructing a large nest of vegetation that stands up to 1 m (3 ft) tall. She will lay and incubate her eggs in the nest.

Female potter wasps build unique pot-shaped nests from mud and water. Once completed, the wasps fill the nests with live insects for their young to feast on.

FIND THE SEAHORSES

Drifting in the branches of a coral called a sea fan, four pygmy seahorses are all but invisible. Not much longer than a thumbnail, these tiny animals have only their amazing camouflage for protection against predators. They spend their lives in one small area, where their colour and knobbly skin exactly match the coral.

The unique pattern on the disc was originally mistaken for an ancient seal.

A large disc-shaped abdomen works as a stopper to block the burrow from predators.

Which spider can plug its burrow?

Chinese hourglass spiders do not trap insects in a web. Instead, these artful arachnids **craft underground burrows**, which they protect with a **specially evolved abdomen**.

The spider's eight short, stocky legs are covered in hairs that sense vibrations caused by animals moving nearby.

ABOVE GROUND

Although pictured here in the open air, the Chinese hourglass spider spends most of its time in a burrow. The spider's name is derived from the Greek "kyklos" meaning "circle", and "kosmeo" meaning "to adorn".

The **Chinese hourglass spider** plugs its burrow **with its body** when danger is near.

📈 FAST FACTS

If the Chinese hourglass spider's burrow is approached by a predator, such as a shrew, the 2.5-cm (1-in) long spider rushes down its burrow and plugs the entrance with its abdomen.

The Chinese hourglass spider is a type of trapdoor spider that can use a burrow in two clever ways. It can hide inside the burrow to catch unsuspecting prey above. Or, if it is threatened by a predator, its flat abdomen works like a stopper to keep the burrow safely closed.

Shrew approaches   Spider hides in burrow

Pandas in the wild

Native to the remote mountain forests of southwest China, giant pandas were declared an endangered species in the 1970s. At this time, there were just over 1,000 pandas left in the wild – a direct result of mass deforestation that had devastated their lush-green home.

Once one of the rarest animals on Earth, pandas reach 125 kg (275 lb) in weight and 1.5 m (5 ft) in length. Although they are skilled climbers and swimmers, they spend nearly all day eating bamboo – a tough, thick grass that makes up most of their diet.

Since 1999, **42 cubs** have also been **raised in zoos** in the USA, Thailand, Spain, Mexico, Austria, and Japan.

In 1981, the Chinese government started working with the World Wide Fund for Nature to help boost the population of panda bears. This included preserving forests, creating vast panda reserves, and teaching communities to harvest bamboo without depleting bamboo supplies. These conservation projects proved successful, and by 2014 there were 1,864 wild pandas. There is still a long way to go, but ongoing efforts are in place to keep these beautiful creatures alive.

BACK · FROM · THE · BRINK

CONSERVATION

Safe space
This healthy young panda, and others like it, are protected in China's Wolong Nature Reserve.

The green turtle takes its name from a layer of green-coloured fat beneath its shell, the result of a diet of marine plants.

The reef stretches for around 2,300 km (1,430 miles) along the coast.

GREAT BARRIER REEF

The Great Barrier Reef is made up of only seven per cent coral. The rest is seagrass, mangroves, sand, and ocean more than 250 km (155 miles) offshore. It is also home to amazing aquatic life, including more than 1,500 species of fish.

What's the biggest living thing?

Australia's **Great Barrier Reef** is the **largest structure** ever built by **living organisms**, known as coral polyps. It covers **344,400 sq km** (133,000 sq miles) and is **visible from space**.

The area of the **Great Barrier Reef** is about the same size as Italy.

The reef makes a barrier between the Australian coastline and the Coral Sea, hence its name.

CORAL BLEACHING

The water in the Great Barrier Reef is warming due to the effects of climate change. As a result, algae that grows in the coral is expelled, turning the coral white — a process known as bleaching. As coral depends on algae for food, it dies without it.

ITALY

The giant clam weighs up to 225 kg (500 lb) and can live for around 100 years. It consumes food produced by billions of algae that live in its tissue.

Threadfin butterfly fish travel around the reef in pairs, feeding on hard and soft corals, as well as worms and sponges.

Creatures of the deep

The **deep, dark oceans** are freezing **cold**, with intense **pressure** and little food. Animals have **adapted** in **unique** ways to **survive**.

Vampire squid
Living 3,000 m (9,800 ft) underwater where there is little oxygen, this 28-cm (11-in) long cephalopod preserves energy by drifting. It forms an umbrella shape with its webbed arms.

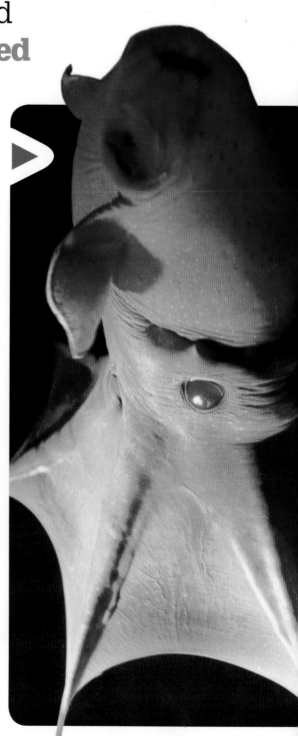

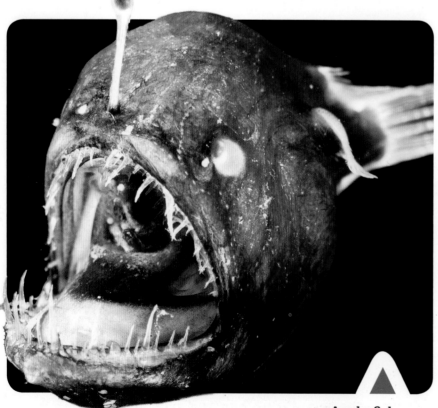

Anglerfish
A female anglerfish lights up the gloom of the deep Atlantic and Antarctic oceans with a glowing spiny growth above her gaping mouth. The light attracts prey.

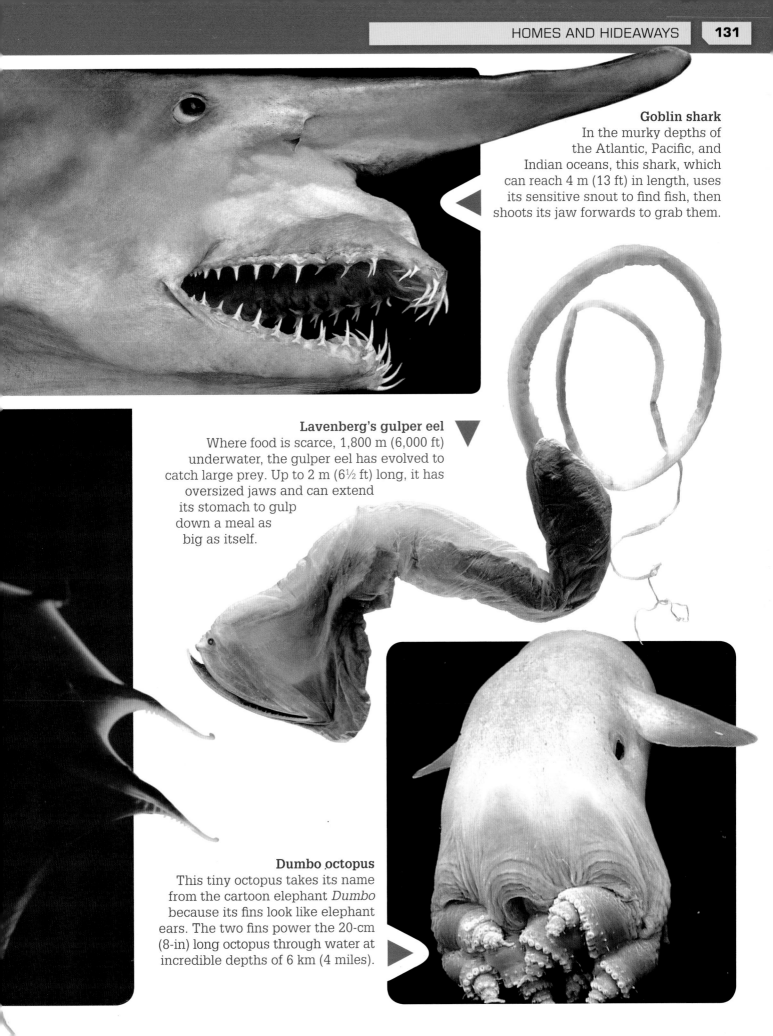

Goblin shark
In the murky depths of the Atlantic, Pacific, and Indian oceans, this shark, which can reach 4 m (13 ft) in length, uses its sensitive snout to find fish, then shoots its jaw forwards to grab them.

Lavenberg's gulper eel
Where food is scarce, 1,800 m (6,000 ft) underwater, the gulper eel has evolved to catch large prey. Up to 2 m (6½ ft) long, it has oversized jaws and can extend its stomach to gulp down a meal as big as itself.

Dumbo octopus
This tiny octopus takes its name from the cartoon elephant *Dumbo* because its fins look like elephant ears. The two fins power the 20-cm (8-in) long octopus through water at incredible depths of 6 km (4 miles).

MYSTERIOUS WEB

This delicate structure is, in fact, a web – the outer "fence" is thought to protect the central silk cone. A student first saw this web in Ecuador in 2013 and watched small, orange spiderlings (below) hatch from a cone. Scientists are working to identify the spiders that spin these unusual webs.

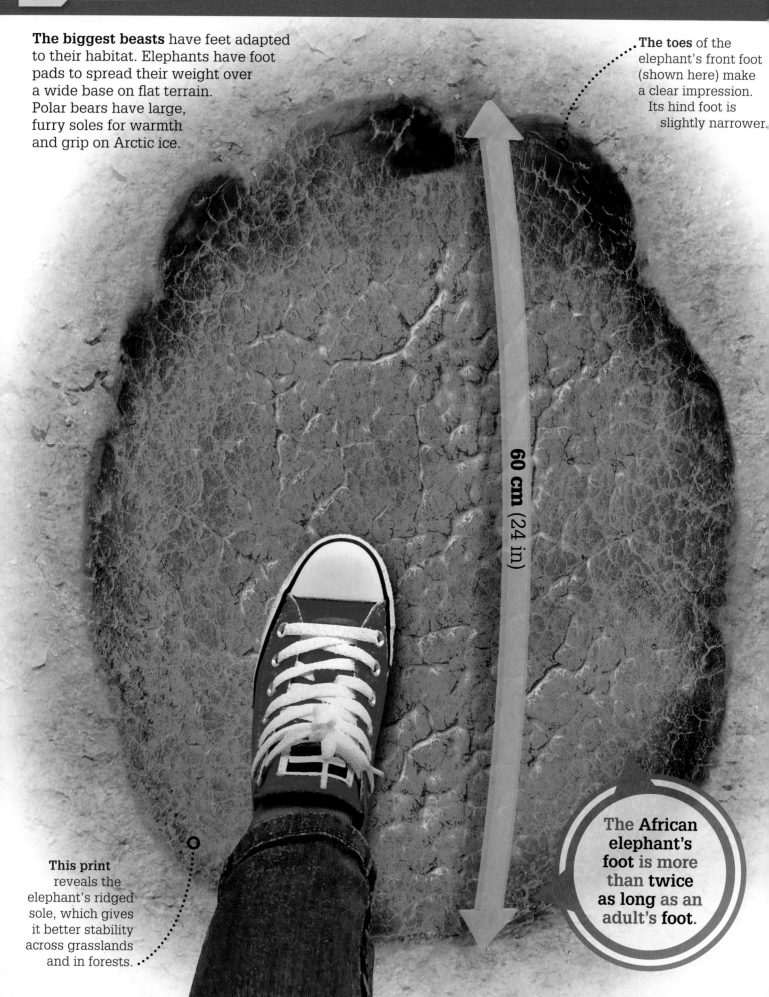

The biggest beasts have feet adapted to their habitat. Elephants have foot pads to spread their weight over a wide base on flat terrain. Polar bears have large, furry soles for warmth and grip on Arctic ice.

The toes of the elephant's front foot (shown here) make a clear impression. Its hind foot is slightly narrower.

60 cm (24 in)

This print reveals the elephant's ridged sole, which gives it better stability across grasslands and in forests.

The African elephant's foot is more than twice as long as an adult's foot.

What animal has the biggest feet?

The **African bush elephant**, the **heaviest creature** on land, also has the world's **largest feet**. These massive pads act as **weight-bearing supports** for its 7,000-kg (15,430-lb) body.

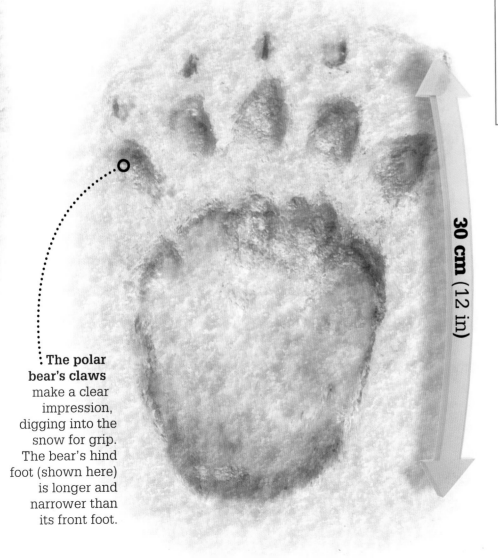

The polar bear's claws make a clear impression, digging into the snow for grip. The bear's hind foot (shown here) is longer and narrower than its front foot.

30 cm (12 in)

WALKING ON WATER

The jacana is a tropical wader with incredibly long legs, toes, and claws. These help spread the bird's weight over a wide area, allowing it to walk on floating vegetation such as water lilies while foraging for insects, fish, and worms.

An average teenager's hand is just under half the length of a polar bear's hind foot. Polar bears, which are found in snowy places such as Canada and Russia, have hairs and creases on their feet to provide traction (grip) on the slippery ice.

CLEAN LIVING

In Singapore, a clean-up campaign has seen the return of smooth-coated otters to the city's rivers. These once toxic waterways have now become a safe home not only for otters, but some fish, too.

Peregrine falcons have made North American and British cities their home, nesting on high-rise buildings and preying on pigeons.

Crab-eating macaques have taken over the Thai city of Lopburi, to the delight of locals, who worship them as a reincarnation of the Hindu monkey god Hanuman.

Wild boars are among the most invasive species, causing chaos and raiding the rubbish in European and Asian cities.

In the busy German capital of **Berlin**, there are roughly **3,000 wild boars**.

Towns and their suburbs present a land of opportunity for wildlife. However, an unhealthy diet based on fast food and waste disposal can cause obesity. Some creatures cause damage and bring disease, making them very unwelcome visitors.

Why do wild animals move to cities?

The **destruction of natural habitats** due to **growing cities** and modern farming methods has driven many **animals into cities**. Here, they **scavenge** for food waste on streets and in parks.

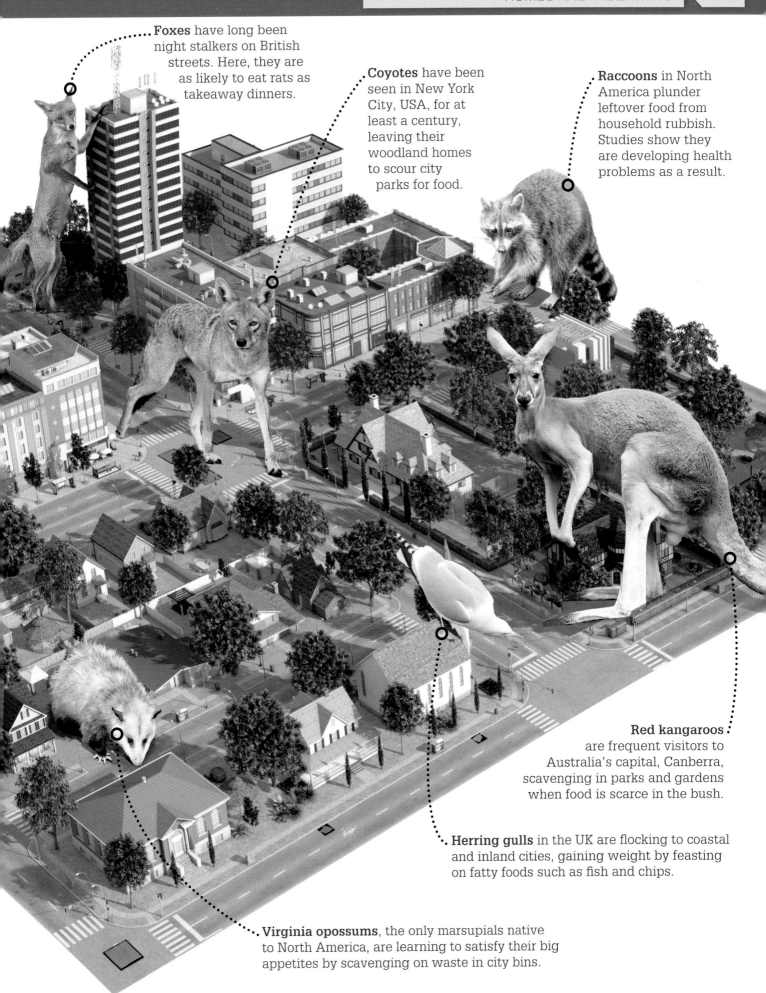

Foxes have long been night stalkers on British streets. Here, they are as likely to eat rats as takeaway dinners.

Coyotes have been seen in New York City, USA, for at least a century, leaving their woodland homes to scour city parks for food.

Raccoons in North America plunder leftover food from household rubbish. Studies show they are developing health problems as a result.

Red kangaroos are frequent visitors to Australia's capital, Canberra, scavenging in parks and gardens when food is scarce in the bush.

Herring gulls in the UK are flocking to coastal and inland cities, gaining weight by feasting on fatty foods such as fish and chips.

Virginia opossums, the only marsupials native to North America, are learning to satisfy their big appetites by scavenging on waste in city bins.

Homes and hideaways facts

GIANT *COCOON*

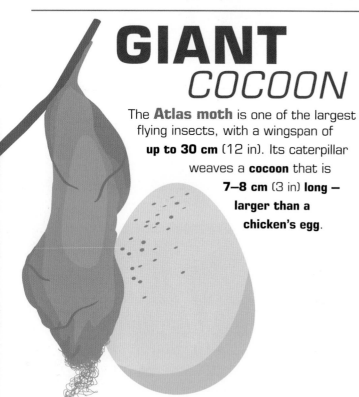

The **Atlas moth** is one of the largest flying insects, with a wingspan of **up to 30 cm** (12 in). Its caterpillar weaves a **cocoon** that is **7–8 cm** (3 in) **long — larger than a chicken's egg.**

TERMIGHTY MOUNDS

• An area of **termite mounds** discovered in Brazil covered **230,000 km²** (88,803 square miles). Some of the mounds date to nearly **4,000 years ago**, when the ancient Egyptians were still building pyramids.

• A **record-breaking termite mound** in the Republic of the Congo reached **12.5 m** (41 ft) above ground — more than **six times the height** of an adult human.

BIGGEST BIRD HOMES

▼ Two **bald eagles** built the world's **largest nest**. It measured **2.9 m** (9½ ft) wide – the same length as a motorcycle – and **6 m** (20 ft) deep. It was estimated to weigh up to **2 tonnes**.

▲ **Malleefowl birds** make the largest egg incubation mounds made of mud, and the biggest weigh up to **300 tonnes** — the same as a **747 jumbo jet**.

▼ **Sociable weaver birds** can fill a whole tree with **one big nest** for up to **400 birds**. The nest can be **4 m** (13 ft) high.

WONDER WEB

The largest spider web ever recorded was woven by a **Darwin's bark spider** and measured **25 m** (82 ft) across — the length of **three African bush elephants**.

CAPTIVE SURVIVAL

Around two-thirds of species of Pacific Partula snails were wiped out by an introduced carnivorous snail. Some were **bred in captivity** – and in 2019, two were returned to their island homeland.

POPULAR PETS

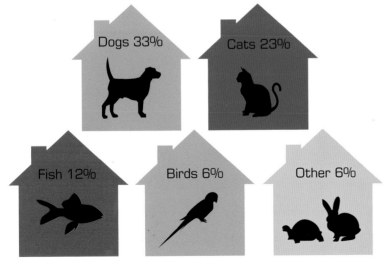

Dogs 33%

Cats 23%

Fish 12%

Birds 6%

Other 6%

A 2016 global survey showed that **more people own dogs** than any other pet. Of the 22 countries surveyed, people in **Argentina** had the highest percentage of pet ownership, at **82%**.

DIGGING DEEP UNDERGROUND

Burrows provide **protection** from enemies and extreme temperatures. Many animals dig homes in the ground, but some species **dig deeper** than others.

- **Cicada**
(2.5 m/8 ft)
A cicada nymph digs and lives in a burrow until it emerges as an adult.

- **Red fox**
(3 m/10 ft)
A red fox digs a hole in winter for spring, when cubs are born in the burrow.

- **Yellow-spotted monitor lizard**
(3.6 m/12 ft)
This Australian reptile digs a corkscrew-shaped tunnel to a nest chamber.

- **European badger**
(4 m/13 ft)
Setts are burrows dug with a badger's long claws and wide feet.

Growing and breeding

For all life on Earth, the urge to grow and breed is overwhelming. Unless animals create new generations of their own kind, their species will die out. To ensure survival, they adopt all kinds of unusual strategies to find a mate, produce offspring, and keep on growing.

Pygmy devil rays gather in vast shoals, numbering in the thousands, in the warm waters of the Gulf of California, Mexico. The rays leap out of the water and belly flop back into the ocean in astonishing acrobatic displays that scientists believe may be intended to attract a mate.

Milly is half the height of the average chihuahua, and could fit on a teaspoon when she was born in 2011.

Milly is known for sticking her tiny tongue out at photographers!

Great Dane Freddy holds the current world record for the tallest dog at 1.04 m (3 ft 5 in).

Milly weighs only 500 g (1 lb 2 oz). She is so small her owner needs to be careful not to lose her at home on the Caribbean island of Puerto Rico.

Which is the smallest dog in the world?

Cheeky **chihuahua Milly** is living proof that good things come in small packages. This super cute canine is the **smallest dog in the world** today, standing just **9.65 cm** (3¾ in) tall.

Milly is only **slightly taller than** a **standard tennis ball**.

A standard tennis ball is 6.7 cm (2½ in) tall.

Milly is so small it would take 10 of her to reach the height of Great Dane Freddy, the world's tallest dog alive today. Researchers have yet to discover the reason for Milly's miniature size.

📊 FAST FACTS

Some breeds of the same species can grow to very different sizes.

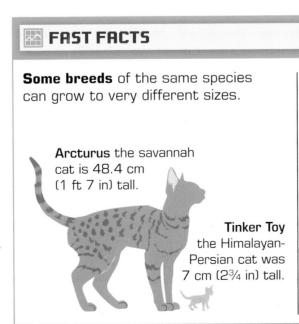

Arcturus the savannah cat is 48.4 cm (1 ft 7 in) tall.

Tinker Toy the Himalayan-Persian cat was 7 cm (2¾ in) tall.

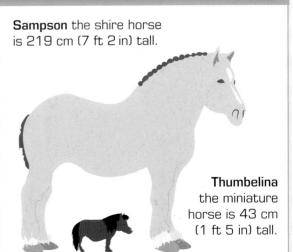

Sampson the shire horse is 219 cm (7 ft 2 in) tall.

Thumbelina the miniature horse is 43 cm (1 ft 5 in) tall.

What animal grows smaller?

In most life cycles, creatures grow bigger until they reach full size. The **paradoxical frog** is an exception to this rule, as the **giant tadpole shrinks** to become a much **smaller frog**.

A very long tail, making up three-quarters of this unusual tadpole's body, grows longer and longer over four months.

Tadpoles are greenish when newly hatched, turning a darker, mottled green that helps them to hide as they grow.

FIRST FOR FROGLETS

There is no tadpole stage for the *Oreophryne* frog from Papua New Guinea. Instead, the father frog protects the eggs against predators until they hatch into full-size froglets.

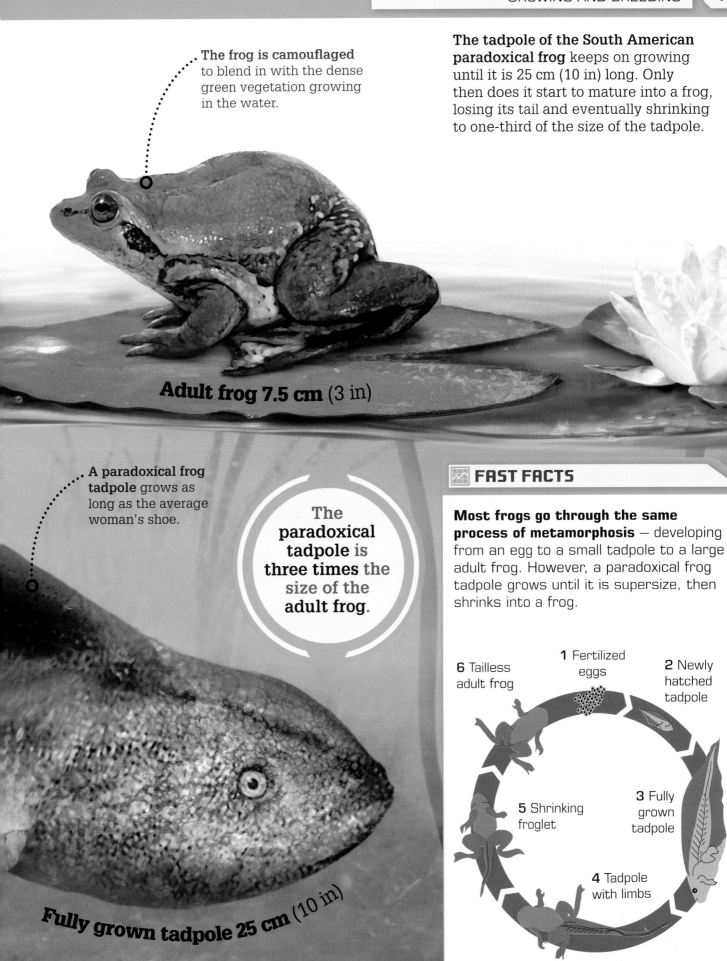

The frog is camouflaged to blend in with the dense green vegetation growing in the water.

The tadpole of the South American paradoxical frog keeps on growing until it is 25 cm (10 in) long. Only then does it start to mature into a frog, losing its tail and eventually shrinking to one-third of the size of the tadpole.

Adult frog 7.5 cm (3 in)

A paradoxical frog tadpole grows as long as the average woman's shoe.

The **paradoxical tadpole is three times the size of the adult frog.**

Fully grown tadpole 25 cm (10 in)

FAST FACTS

Most frogs go through the same process of metamorphosis — developing from an egg to a small tadpole to a large adult frog. However, a paradoxical frog tadpole grows until it is supersize, then shrinks into a frog.

1 Fertilized eggs

2 Newly hatched tadpole

3 Fully grown tadpole

4 Tadpole with limbs

5 Shrinking froglet

6 Tailless adult frog

What is the hungriest animal?

Although small in stature, the **Eurasian pygmy shrew** is big in appetite. This **tiny mammal** eats **125 per cent** of its **body weight** in food every day.

SNAKE SNACK

Measuring 4.5 m (15 ft) in length, the Burmese python can swallow a whole deer or crocodile in one go. After eating such huge prey, the python can survive without food for a month.

The heart of a pygmy shrew beats 1,200 times a minute to maintain the shrew's high metabolism. A human heart rate is 15 times slower, at 80 beats a minute.

This shrew measures 90 mm (3½ in) in length and weighs 3 g (⅛ oz), which is lighter than a piece of paper.

An **adult human** would have to munch **387 sandwiches a day** to match the **shrew**.

More than 250 small arthropods, including beetles, flies, and spiders, are eaten by this warm-blooded hunter every day to provide it with the energy it needs.

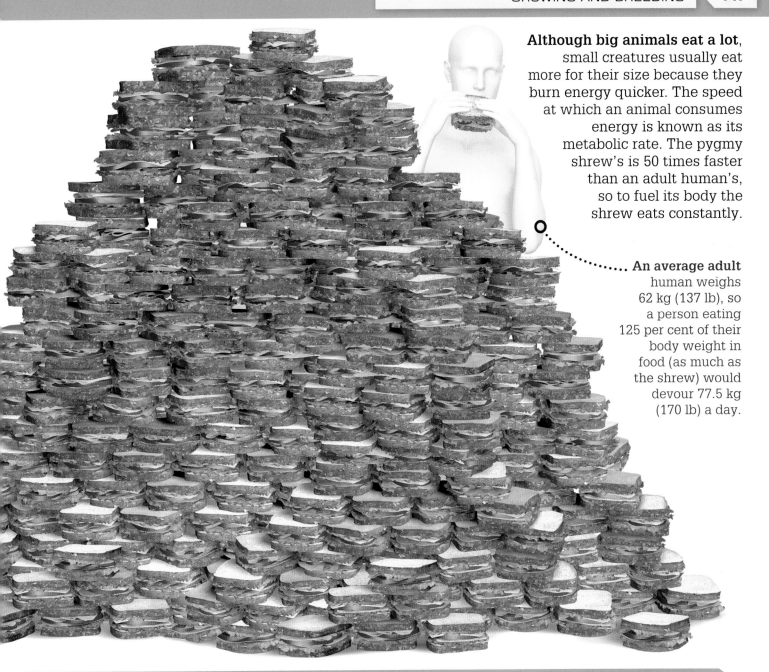

Although big animals eat a lot, small creatures usually eat more for their size because they burn energy quicker. The speed at which an animal consumes energy is known as its metabolic rate. The pygmy shrew's is 50 times faster than an adult human's, so to fuel its body the shrew eats constantly.

An average adult human weighs 62 kg (137 lb), so a person eating 125 per cent of their body weight in food (as much as the shrew) would devour 77.5 kg (170 lb) a day.

 **FAST FACTS**

A blue whale weighing around 150 tonnes can eat six tonnes of krill every day.

Giant pandas eat fibrous bamboo shoots and leaves for up to 16 hours a day.

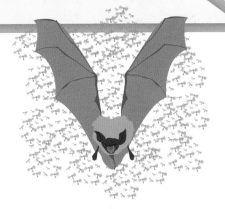

Little brown bats can eat up to 1,000 mosquitoes an hour, hunting constantly at night.

A broad-tailed hummingbird can flap its wings 70–80 times per second, allowing it to hover and perform acrobatics. The bird, which weighs just 3.5 g (0.1 oz), needs a lot of energy to fuel its flight. This comes from the nectar it drinks.

A hummingbird's heart beats around 500 times a minute at rest, increasing to 1,300 times a minute when hovering.

NECTAR POINTS

In return for a flower's nectar, most hummingbirds pollinate plants, picking up pollen from one flower and taking it to the next. Some visit up to 2,000 flowers a day. However, the wedge-billed hummingbird drills into the nectar bulb at the base of a plant, getting nectar without pollen.

More than half the nectar a **hummingbird drinks is sugar**. Sugar makes up 10 per cent of cola, so to ingest the same ratio of sugar to body weight, a person would have to drink 250 litres (66 gallons).

An **adult** would have to gulp **750 cans of cola a day** to get a hummingbird's sugar fix.

FAST FACTS

There are more than 300 species of hummingbird, all native to the Americas.

The rufous hummingbird migrates up to 4,828 km (3,000 miles), from Alaska to Mexico.

The Cuban bee hummingbird is the world's smallest bird. At 5.7 cm (2¼ in) long, it can perch on a pencil.

Life-size

How much **nectar** do **hummingbirds** drink?

A **hummingbird** drinks **one-and-a-half times its weight** in sugary **nectar** a day. To slurp as much **sugar** for their size, a **person** would have to drink a **can of cola** every **two minutes**.

What animal has a supersize brood?

From **one to hundreds of millions**, every species in the animal kingdom has its own number of **eggs or young**. The **ocean sunfish** is the ultimate mother, spawning up to **300 million eggs** in one go.

Orangutan mothers can spend nine years caring for one baby, making it the longest time between births of any mammal.

Some animals have few offspring and spend years looking after them. Others lay vast numbers of eggs or give birth to many young, but abandon them to survive on their own.

Female grey partridges lay more eggs in one go than any other bird. Both parents raise the fledgling birds.

Tailless tenrecs are tiny, spiny mammals from Madagascar. They give birth to one large litter a year, but only half the young survive the first month.

Sumatran orangutan
One baby every nine years

Grey partridge
24 eggs per clutch

Tailless tenrec
32 young per litter

FAST FACTS

An Australian ghost moth can lay more than 29,000 eggs in one clutch, dropping them while in flight in a scatter-bomb effect.

A three-toed skink can produce both eggs and live young in the same brood. This is unusual, as most lizards do either one or the other.

Sandtiger shark pups fight each other for survival in the womb, using their embryonic teeth to kill and eat their siblings. Only one — the strongest — is born from each litter.

The **ocean sunfish lays** the **largest number of eggs** of any **vertebrate**.

Ocean sunfish lay millions of eggs, but the eggs' tiny size and the fact that they are scattered in the sea mean their chances of survival are low.

Blue sharks have some of the largest litters of any animal, but predators eat many of the pups in infancy.

Hawksbill sea turtles lay more eggs than any other reptile, but hatchlings risk their lives to migrate from nests in the sand to the sea.

Blue shark
135 pups per litter

Hawksbill turtle
242 eggs per clutch

Ocean sunfish
300 million eggs per spawning

MASS SPAWNING

Every year, common frogs lay their eggs in billowing masses of jelly called frogspawn. Frogs often share breeding sites, producing tens of thousands of eggs between them. Each black dot in the jelly is an egg that may grow into a tadpole. Only a tiny number hatch, as predators such as fish and insects devour the spawn.

What's the oddest couple?

Males of many species are **bigger than females**. In **elephant seals** this size difference is **massive**. However, in other animals it's the other way round.

SIZE MATTERS

At 8 cm (3 in) long, the female golden silk spider can be six times the size of the tiny male. Females have evolved to be larger so they can lay more eggs and make strong webs to catch insects to nourish them.

The enormous male, called the beachmaster, is the dominant partner of up to 50 small females.

A female elephant seal is one-fifth of the male's weight.

The tiny females lose one-third of their body weight while suckling their seal pups. They don't eat for a month while nursing.

Southern elephant seals are the largest species of seal. Males measure up to 5 m (16 ft) long and can weigh 3,000 kg (6,600 lb). By contrast, their female partners may be only 3 m (9 ft 10 in) long and weigh just 600 kg (1,323 lb). The Antarctic waters provide a rich diet of fish and squid to maintain their blubber.

FAST FACTS

Male viper

Female viper

Male parrot

Female parrot

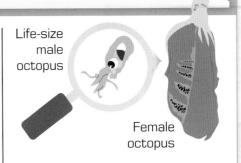

Life-size male octopus

Female octopus

Wagler's pit vipers show a clear difference between the sexes: males are thin and bright green, while females are thick, longer, and banded.

Eclectus parrots are proof that opposites attract: males are vibrant green with yellow beaks, while females are bright red with black beaks.

A female blanket octopus weighs 40,000 times more than a male, and grows 1.8 m (6 ft) long, while the male reaches just 2.5 cm (1 in).

Its trunk-like nose and massive size have earned this species the name elephant seal.

The bulky body, powerful flippers, and strong teeth are used in aggressive fights with other males for female partners.

Which parent gives its life for its young?

Proud parents may say they would do anything for their children, but **black lace-weaver spiders** actually let their **offspring eat them alive!**

> Spiderlings eat their mother alive, sucking the juices from her body.

Female black lace-weaver spiders have a short life because the spiderlings eat their mother three days after hatching.

African caecilians

Worm-like amphibian caecilian mothers allow new babies to eat their fatty, nutrient-rich skin, which regrows.

Italian scorpions

Scorpion mothers carry hundreds of soft-bodied scorplings on their backs, protecting the young with the sting in their tail.

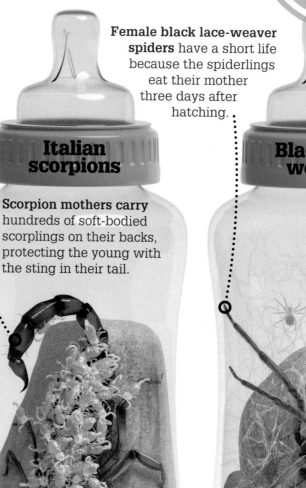

Black lace-weavers

Across the animal kingdom, parents adopt unusual strategies to give their young a head start in life. From mothers eaten by their children to fathers giving birth, some species go to great lengths to ensure their families continue for generations to come.

FAMILY FAVOURITE

Female giant pandas often give birth to twin cubs, born blind and hairless. The mother may choose to raise only one cub. In captive breeding, the abandoned twin is cared for in an incubator.

Jawfish fathers hold the mother's eggs in their mouth until hatching time, going without food for up to 10 days.

Seahorse fathers hatch eggs laid by the mother in a pouch on the male's stomach, using contractions to give birth to up to 2,000 live young.

Hundreds of Surinam toad eggs are embedded in the skin of the mother's back, later erupting as toadlets. The mother is unharmed.

Yellow-headed jawfish

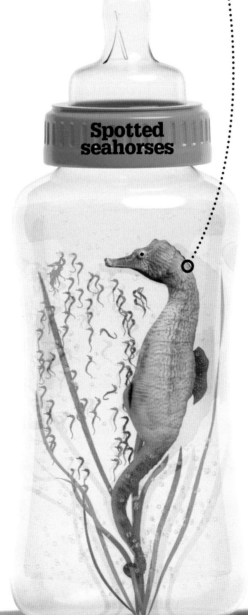

Spotted seahorses

Surinam toads

Sandy survivor

Herds of Arabian oryx, with their spectacular horns up to 1.5 m (5 ft) long, were once a familiar sight throughout the sandy deserts of the Arabian Peninsula.

Sadly, in the 19th and 20th centuries the horns of this beautiful antelope made a tempting target for hunters. In 1972, the last Arabian oryx disappeared from the wild. Just a handful of animals remained in zoos or were kept in privately owned herds.

Today, more than 1,200 Arabian oryx thrive in the wild, and about 6,000–7,000 live in captivity.

With the prospect of the Arabian oryx vanishing forever, an international conservation effort led by the World Wide Fund for Nature, together with several zoos, made plans for its rescue. Under this scheme, called Operation Oryx, the conservationists bred the antelope in captivity, building up new herds that were gradually reintroduced into the wild. The success story continues, as Arabian oryx are now protected by law and their numbers are slowly rising.

BACK · FROM · THE · BRINK

CONSERVATION

Desert life
The Arabian oryx can survive for weeks without water. Its broad hooves allow it to walk on shifting sands without sinking in. The smaller animal seen nearby is a gazelle, which shares the oryx's desert home.

Courtship displays

In search of the perfect partner, showstopping male birds **parade** and **serenade** females with **dazzling courtship displays** and **songs**.

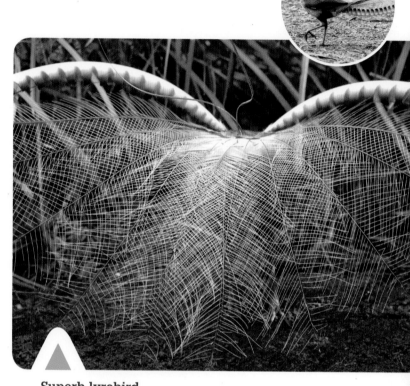

Superb lyrebird
The male of this Australian songbird builds a mound on which to stand and showcase his spectacular fan of tail feathers, all the while singing loudly to catch the attention of a female.

Magnificent frigatebird
The male of this tropical American seabird inflates a red pouch on his throat and emits a shrill trill to attract a female. The pair then perform an acrobatic aerial display together before mating.

Greater bird of paradise
The colourful males of this bird of paradise from New Guinea compete for females in special displays on parade grounds known as leks. Up to 15 males perch on a tree branch, hopping up and down, lifting their tail feathers, flapping their wings, and calling out to attract attention. The female chooses the one that puts on the best show.

Temminck's tragopan
The male of this Chinese pheasant inflates a brilliant blue and red bib under its beak and two fleshy horns on its head, while bobbing and flapping its wings. This is a captivating sight for the female, who has only dull grey plumage.

Satin bowerbird
The male satin bowerbird of Australia, with his glossy blue plumage and violet eyes, spares no effort to attract a mate. He builds a structure known as a bower out of twigs, decorating it with blue objects such as feathers and plastic. He then struts around it to impress the small, green female.

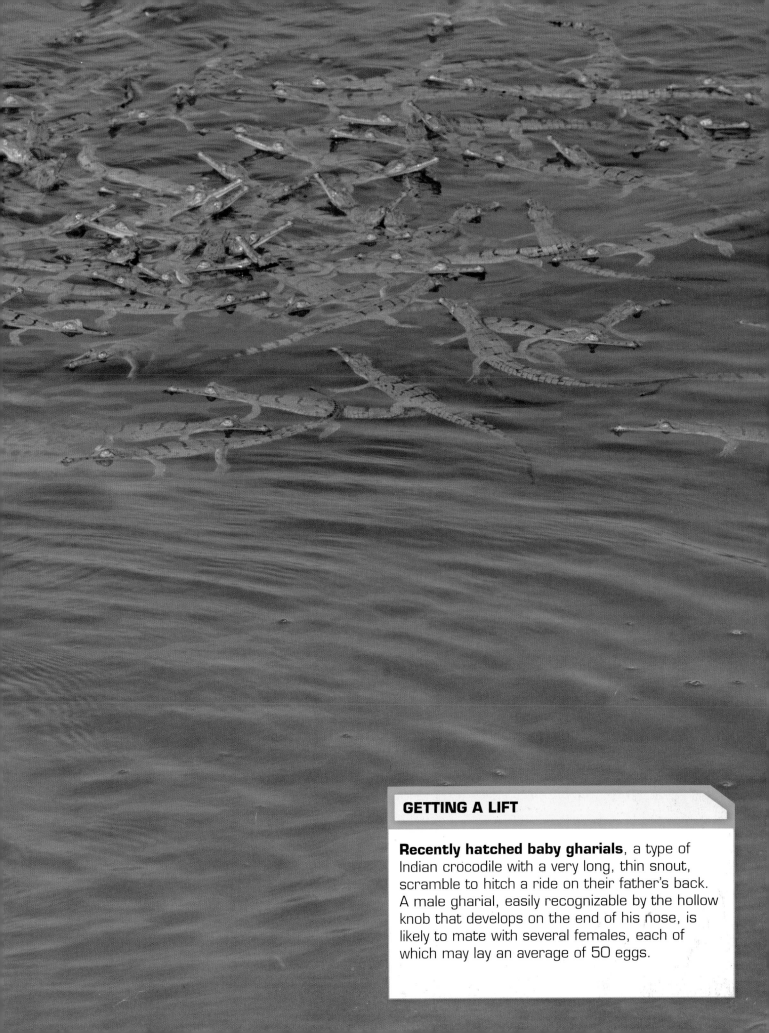

GETTING A LIFT

Recently hatched baby gharials, a type of Indian crocodile with a very long, thin snout, scramble to hitch a ride on their father's back. A male gharial, easily recognizable by the hollow knob that develops on the end of his nose, is likely to mate with several females, each of which may lay an average of 50 eggs.

SELF-RENEWING SALAMANDER

Another champion at self-renewal is the axolotl, a type of salamander. Not only can this aquatic animal regrow its limbs and tail, it can also renew damaged parts of vital internal organs, such as the brain, heart, and lungs.

Starfish

Five-armed starfish are the most common, but some have 10, 20, and even 40 arms. These animals are also known as sea stars.

A new starfish, with a body and all its limbs, can grow from one severed arm.

When a starfish's arm becomes detached, it may sprout a new body and new arms. These budding arms will continue to grow until they reach the same size as the original arm.

A starfish's eyes are located at the tips of its arms. Many of its other organs are also contained in the arms.

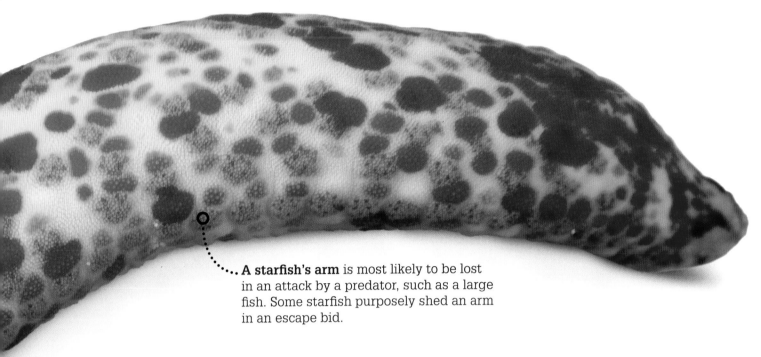

A starfish's arm is most likely to be lost in an attack by a predator, such as a large fish. Some starfish purposely shed an arm in an escape bid.

What **animal** can grow a **new body?**

Grow-your-own **body parts** may be far in the future for humans, but not for **starfish**, which can **replace lost arms**. Incredibly, a cut-off arm sometimes grows into a whole **new** starfish.

FAST FACTS

An arm severed from a starfish through injury can sometimes grow into a completely new starfish. This can happen only if vital pieces of the original body are still attached to the arm.

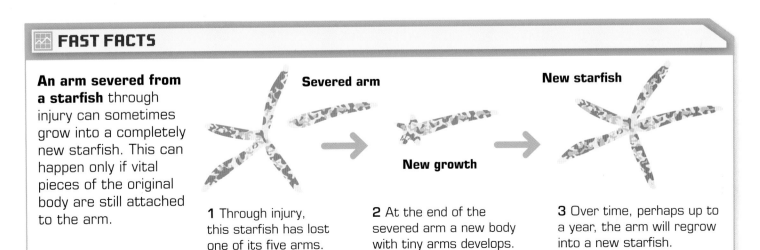

Severed arm

New growth

New starfish

1 Through injury, this starfish has lost one of its five arms.

2 At the end of the severed arm a new body with tiny arms develops.

3 Over time, perhaps up to a year, the arm will regrow into a new starfish.

What animal is a living fossil?

The **nautilus** of today shares many features with its ancestors, **prehistoric nautiloids**. It has changed so little over time that it is known as a **living fossil**.

400 million years ago...

Prehistoric nautiloids, such as *Charactoceras*, had smooth, coiled shells, much like today's nautilus.

Dunkleosteus was a fierce, bony-plated fish that lived in the late Devonian period, nearly 400 million years ago.

Stethacanthus was a shark-like fish with a distinctive dorsal fin. It died out more than 300 million years ago.

Today's **nautilus** has barely changed in almost **half a billion years**.

ENDURING CRAB

Horseshoe crab fossils have been found from 445 million years ago, revealing that the species has remained virtually unchanged since then. This crab's tough shell has enabled it to survive mass extinctions.

The chambered nautilus shows striking physical similarities to fossil finds from 400 million years ago – long before the dinosaurs and when almost all complex animal life lived in the oceans. It is a relative of squids and octopuses. Together, they make up a group of molluscs called cephalopods.

Ninety thin tentacles are attached to the 25-cm (10-in) long body of the nautilus. The tentacles grab prey such as crabs, while the horny beak bites through shells.

The nautilus lives inside a shell, using air chambers in the shell to stay afloat and jet propulsion to move through the tropical waters of the Indian and Pacific oceans.

...and today!

Triggerfish swim with nautiluses today.

Growing and breeding facts

ANIMALS
WITH AMAZING GROWTH

▼ Panda
Cubs at birth weigh about **100 g** (4 oz), barely **one-thousandth** of their mother's weight of **100–115 kg** (220–250 lb).

▲ Red kangaroo
Baby kangroos, or "joeys", are very **undeveloped** when born and weigh just **1 g** ($^1/_3$ oz), but they **may reach 90 kg** (200 lb) when adult.

▶ Blue whale
Calves are **big** babies, weighing up to **2,700 kg** (6,000 lb) at birth, but the **adults weigh** up to **150,000 kg** (330,000 lb).

GOING HUNGRY

Not eating for hours makes anyone feel hungry but some animals can **miss meals for years**. If food is scarce or temperatures extreme, their body processes, such as heart rate, slow down and they live in suspended animation.

- **Olm** (a salamander): may survive **10 years**
- **African lungfish**: may survive **5 years**
- **Royal python**: may survive **2 years**

GIGANTIC
GRUB

Goliath beetles from Africa, the world's heaviest insects, weigh around **60 g** (2 oz) as **adults**. Their **larvae**, almost too big to hold in a hand, are nearly **twice as heavy**, tipping the scales at up to **100 g** (4 oz).

LONG-TERM LARVA

Golden jewel beetles hold the record for long development. Some have lasted an **incredible 51 years** as **larvae** before emerging as adults.

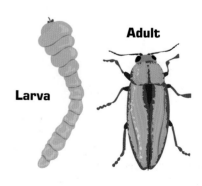

Adult

Larva

MUMS IN WAITING

Many animals have much **longer pregnancies** than humans. This means their **babies** are **well developed**, which gives them the best possible chance of **survival** in the wild.

• **Alpine salamander**: **Pregnancy 2–3 years** Unlike most amphibians, they have **live young**, instead of eggs that might **not hatch** in the cold.

• **Elephant**: **Pregnancy 22 months** The babies **rely on** their **mums** a lot but they can **walk** soon after birth.

• **Giraffe**: **Pregnancy 15 months** A **one-day-old** calf can **run** from danger.

• **Human**: **Pregnancy 9 months** A newborn baby is **helpless** and needs a mother's **care for years**.

LONGEST EGG INCUBATION

• **Emperor penguin**: **65–75 days** For all this time the **female leaves** the male with their **one egg** while she goes off to feed at sea. The **male eats nothing**.

• **Wandering albatross**: **77 days** Both parents **share egg-minding**, each **taking turns** on the nest for two–three weeks.

• **Northern brown kiwi**: **up to 92 days** The **male** sits on one or two eggs, which are **huge** in proportion to a kiwi's size.

• **Octopus**: **4.5 years** This is the **longest** known time for an animal to **brood** eggs.

NOT FUSSY EATERS

Some animals, known as **omnivores**, eat a mixed diet that includes both **meat** and **plant foods**. Four are shown here, with their favourite menus.

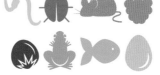

• **Black bears** will eat **grasses**, roots, berries, insects, **fish**, small mammals, and even **human leftovers**.

• **Snapping turtles** munch **worms**, snails, insects, crustaceans, waterweeds, **fruit**, frogs, and **snakes**.

• **Raccoons** tuck in to insects, worms, small animals such as **mice**, fruit, nuts, fish, frogs, and **bird's eggs**.

• **Chimpanzees** like **fruit** and leaves best, but they also eat seeds, nuts, and flowers, plus **insects** and other small animals.

GLOSSARY

The words listed here, which can be found throughout this book, are all used to describe animals and the world they live in.

Abdomen
In back-boned animals, the part of the body that contains the digestive and reproductive organs; in arthropods, it is the rear part after the head and thorax.

Adaptation
The way in which an animal changes its body or behaviour to fit in with its environment.

Amphibian
A back-boned animal that can live both on land andin water, such as a frog, toad, or newt.

Antennae
The pair of sense organs, or feelers, on the heads of insects, such as flies, and crustaceans, such as lobsters and crabs.

Aquatic
Living almost entirely in water.

Arachnid
One of a group of animals, including spiders and scorpions, that have a hard outer skeleton and eight legs.

Arthropod
An animal with a hard outer skeleton and jointed legs. This group includes insects, spiders, and crustaceans.

Blubber
The layer of fat beneath the skin of large sea mammals, including seals and walruses.

Caecilian
A worm-like, legless amphibian that lives mostly underground.

Camouflage
Patterns and colours that protect an animal by making it hard for enemies to see it.

Carnivore
An animal that eats only meat.

Carrion
The rotting flesh of dead animals.

Cephalopod
One of a group of soft-bodied marine animals that include octopuses and squids.

Clutch
All the eggs produced at one time by an animal, including birds, reptile, and fish.

Colony
A group of animals that live closely together, such as ants.

Conservation
Protection of wildlife and habitats to prevent damage or loss.

Crustacean
An animal with a hard outer skeleton, a segmented body, and jointed legs, such as a crab or lobster.

Echolocation
A way of locating objects in air or water by bouncing sound waves off them.

Evolution
The process of change over many generations.

Exoskeleton
The hard external skeleton of animals such as insects, spiders, and crustaceans.

Extinct
No individuals alive.

Fossil
The preserved remains or impressions of a prehistoric animal or plant.

Habitat
The natural home of an animal.

Herbivore
An animal that eats only plants.

Invertebrate
An animal without a backbone, such as an insect.

Iridescent
Having shimmering colours that appear to change when seen from different angles.

Krill
Tiny, shrimp-like animals, found in great numbers in the world's oceans, that provide food for much larger animals, including some whales.

Larva
The early life stage of an animal between an egg and the final adult form. Larvae (plural) include caterpillars and tadpoles.

Litter
The group of young animals that are all born at the same time to the same mother.

Mammal
An animal, usually with fur, that creates its own body heat and feeds its young with milk.

Marsupial
A mammal that typically carries its young in a belly pouch until they can look after themselves.

Metamorphosis
The process of changing from a juvenile form to an adult, such as the transformation from caterpillar to butterfly.

Migration
Seasonal movement of animals to and from breeding or feeding grounds.

Mimicry
A way of fooling predators or prey, when an animal has evolved to look or behave like another animal that is dangerous or not good to eat. Some creatures mimic objects such as leaves or stones.

Mollusc
An invertebrate animal with a soft body and sometimes a protective shell. Slugs, snails, clams, and octopuses are all types of mollusc.

Nectar
Sugary fluid produced by flowers to attract pollen-spreading animals.

Nocturnal
Active at night.

Omnivore
An animal that eats both meat and plants.

Parasite
An animal that lives on or inside another animal, causing harm to the host.

Pigment
A substance that gives something its colour.

Plankton
Small animals and plants that drift in large bodies of water and are a major food source for many aquatic creatures.

Plumage
A bird's feathers.

Predator
An animal that hunts other animals for food.

Prey
An animal that is hunted and eaten by another.

Primates
A group of mammals that includes apes, monkeys, and humans.

Reptile
A back-boned animal, such as a snake, lizard, or crocodile, whose body warmth depends on the temperature of its surroundings.

Savannah
A large, flat area of grassland with few trees that mostly occurs in tropical countries.

Scavenger
An animal that feeds on the rotting remains of dead animals and other matter.

Semiaquatic
Living partly in water and partly on land.

Spawn
The fertilized eggs of animals such as fish and frogs, usually laid in masses.

Species
A group of organisms that can breed with each other and produce offspring like themselves.

Tentacles
Flexible body extensions, such as those on octopuses and jellyfish, used for grasping and sensing.

Venom
A poisonous substance that is injected through bites and stings.

Vertebrate
An animal with a backbone.

INDEX

ACKNOWLEDGMENTS

Dorling Kindersley would like to thank: Victoria Pyke for proofreading; Elizabeth Wise for indexing; Kelsie Besaw, Anna Limerick, and Vicky Richards for editorial assistance; Ann Baggaley for additional writing.

The publisher would like to thank the following for their kind permission to reproduce their photographs:

(Key: a-above; b-below/bottom; c-centre; f-far; l-left; r-right; t-top)

1 Alamy Stock Photo: VDWI Automotive (clb). **Dreamstime. com:** Uckarintra Wongcharit (crb). **2 Alamy Stock Photo:** blickwinkel / Schmidbauer (cra); Gerry Pearce (bc); robertharding / Marco Simoni (c). **Dreamstime.com:** Chernetskaya (cb); Andrii Zastrozhnov (tc). **Professor Maciej Henneberg:** (cb/handprint). **3 Alamy Stock Photo:** blickwinkel (cla). **4 Alamy Stock Photo:** Skip Moody / Rainbow / RGB Ventures / SuperStock (bl). **Dwight Kuhn:** (tr). **naturepl.com:** Bence Mate (tc). **5 Alamy Stock Photo:** Nopadol Uengbunchoo (tc). **Getty Images:** by wildestanimal (tr). **naturepl.com:** Piotr Naskrecki (tl). **6-7 naturepl.com:** Bence Mate. **9 naturepl.com:** Alex Mustard (bc). **11 Alamy Stock Photo:** Nature Picture Library (bc). **12 naturepl. com:** Nature Production (clb). **Heinz Wiesbauer, Vienna:** (c). **12-13 SuperStock:** Minden Pictures. **14-15 Rolland Gelly. 16-17 Mark Cowan. 20 Alamy Stock Photo:** Lisa1234 / Stockimo (bl). **Dreamstime.com:** Andreykuzmin (crb); Chernetskaya (cr); Ulianna19970 (cra); Andrii Zastrozhnov (tr). **iStockphoto.com:** rasikabendre (br). **21 Alamy Stock Photo:** Robert Henno (cra); robertharding / Marco Simoni (cl); Gerry Pearce (bl). **Dreamstime.com:** Chernetskaya (clb/badge, cra/ badge); Andrii Zastrozhnov (tl, tr/ Lanyard). **Professor Maciej Henneberg:** (clb). **Science Photo Library:** Tony Camacho (tr); Sheila Terry (cr). **23 Getty Images:** Justin Sullivan (bl). **24 naturepl.com:** Ingo Arndt (bc). **26 Alamy Stock Photo:** Robert Thompson / Nature Picture Library (crb); **www.pqpictures. co.uk** (bc). **Dorling Kindersley:** Natural History Museum, London (cb). **Dreamstime.com:** Lukas Jonaitis (bl). **naturepl.com:**

Visuals Unlimited (clb). **SuperStock:** Ingo Arndt / Minden Pictures (cl). **27 Alamy Stock Photo:** blickwinkel / fotototo (tc); Nature Photographers Ltd / Paul R. Sterry (tl); blickwinkel / Schmidbauer (tr); Skip Moody / Rainbow / RGB Ventures / SuperStock (cb); Custom Life Science Images (bc). **naturepl. com:** Ingo Arndt (cra). **28-29 Getty Images:** Chris Brunskill Ltd. **30 Alamy Stock Photo:** Daniele Occhiato / Buiten-Beeld (clb). **30-31 Alamy Stock Photo:** Wild Wonders of Europe / Lundgre / Nature Picture Library. **32 123RF.com:** Tawatchai Khid-arn (bl). **32-33 naturepl.com:** Anup Shah. **34 naturepl.com:** Thomas Marent (tl). **36-37 TurboSquid:** 3dThorium. **36 TurboSquid:** PIS88 (clb). **37 Alamy Stock Photo:** Rick & Nora Bowers (br). **39 naturepl.com:** Doug Gimesy (bc). **40 naturepl. com:** Naskrecki & Guyton (tr). **40-41 naturepl.com:** Naskrecki & Guyton. **41 Alamy Stock Photo:** Johner Images (crb). **naturepl. com:** Dietmar Nill (cb). **42 iStockphoto.com:** Stéphane Rochon (bl). **46-47 Dwight Kuhn. 48 TurboSquid:** Praveen Jayasinghe. **49 TurboSquid:** Skazok. **50-51 naturepl.com:** Alex Mustard. **50 naturepl.com:** Alex Mustard (bl). **51 Getty Images:** Gerard Soury (c). **54-55 Dan Abbott. 57 Rex by Shutterstock:** AP (br). **58 Alamy Stock Photo:** Jeff Milisen (cl); Maximilian Weinzierl (b). **59 naturepl.com:** Michael & Patricia Fogden (cl); Thomas Marent (r); Konrad Wothe (cla); Nick Garbutt (cb); Visuals Unlimited (bl). **60 Alamy Stock Photo:** Sean Cameron (tl). **65 naturepl.com:** Pete Oxford (tr). **66 naturepl.com:** Stephen Belcher (bl). **66-67 Alamy Stock Photo:** David Kleyn. **68 Alamy Stock Photo:** Andrey Nekrasov (b); WaterFrame_rok (cr). **69 Alamy Stock Photo:** Andrey Nekrasov (b); WaterFrame_fur (tr). **SuperStock:** Minden Pictures (tl). **70-71 SuperStock:** Paul Bertner / Minden Pictures. **70 naturepl. com:** Paul Bertner (tl). **72 Alamy Stock Photo:** VDWI Automotive (t). **73 Dreamstime.com:** Uckarintra Wongcharit (c). **74-75 Dreamstime.com:** Flynt (frame). **74 Tina Hutchinson** (tr). **naturepl.com:** Brandon Cole (bl); Alex Mustard (tl). **75 Alamy Stock Photo:** Tim Gainey (clb); Alexandra Laube / imageBROKER (crb). **Dreamstime.com:** Maska82 (tl). **SuperStock:** Flip Nicklin /

Minden Pictures (tr). **76-77 Getty Images:** Stephen Frink / Photolibrary. **78 Alamy Stock Photo:** Robert Pickett / Papilio (clb). **78-79 Dreamstime.com:** Otsphoto. **79 Alamy Stock Photo:** Tierfotoagentur / Y. Janetzek (br). **Getty Images:** Tollkühn / ullstein bild (tr). **naturepl.com:** Neil Bromhall (tl). **82-83 Courtesy of Guinness World Records 2019. 83 Dreamstime.com:** Horia Vlad Bogdan / Horiabogdan (crb). **84-85 Shikhei Goh. 90-91 naturepl.com:** Piotr Naskrecki. **93 iStockphoto. com:** E+ / pchoui (bc). **94 Alamy Stock Photo:** Andrey Gudkov (crb). **Getty Images:** Picture by Tambako the Jaguar (bl). **iStockphoto.com:** GP232 / E+ (cl). **95 Alamy Stock Photo:** Christian Vorhofer / imageBROKER (b). **naturepl.com:** Bence Mate (t). **95 naturepl.com:** Bence Mate (t). **96-97 Getty Images:** Alastair Macewen. **98 Alamy Stock Photo:** Frankie Angel (c); Juniors Bildarchiv GmbH / F279 (tl). **imagequestmarine.com:** Peter Batson (c). **Janet M. Storey:** (crb). **98-99 Dreamstime.com:** Alhovik. **99 Alamy Stock Photo:** Doug Allan / Nature Picture Library (tl); Pete Morris / AGAMI Photo Agency (clb); Steve Gschmeissner / Science Photo Library (crb); Fred van Wijk (r). **Dreamstime. com:** Jason Ondreicka (tr); Boris Ryaposov (c). **101 Depositphotos Inc:** yulia-zl18 (bl). **104 123RF. com:** Tawatchai Khid-arn (bl). **104-105 O'Brian Clarisse, Whitetone Films. 106-107 Caters News Agency:** Eko Adiyanto. **106 SuperStock:** Animals Animals (br). **108-109 Kevin Ebi. 110 Alamy Stock Photo:** Action Plus Sports Images (clb). **114-115 Alamy Stock Photo:** Nopadol Uengbunchoo. **117 Alamy Stock Photo:** David Tyrer (t). **118 Alamy Stock Photo:** GZS / imageBROKER (bc); Reinhard Hölzl / imageBROKER (tl). **naturepl.com:** Gavin Maxwell (clb); Xi Zhinong (tr). **119 Alamy Stock Photo:** Jan Sochor (bl). **Science Photo Library:** W K Fletcher (tl). **121 Alamy Stock Photo:** Ronald Wittek / mauritius images GmbH (cra). **122-123 naturepl.com:** Jurgen Freund. **122 naturepl.com:** Jurgen Freund (cla). **123 naturepl.com:** Jurgen Freund (ca, cb). **124-125 Alamy Stock Photo:** blickwinkel. **125 Alamy Stock Photo:** Imaginechina Limited (tr). **126-127 naturepl. com:** Katherine Feng. **126 123RF. com:** Tawatchai Khid-arn (clb). **128 Dorling Kindersley:** David

Peart (tc). **129 Alamy Stock Photo:** Suzanne Long (tr). **Dreamstime. com:** Mirecca (bl). **130 naturepl. com:** Solvin Zankl (cl). **130-131 SuperStock:** Steve Downeranth / Pantheon. **131 Alamy Stock Photo:** NOAA (br). **naturepl.com:** Norbert Wu (c). **SeaPics.com:** © David Shen (tl). **132-133 Alamy Stock Photo:** Anton Sorokin. **133 Rex by Shutterstock:** Solent News (br). **135 naturepl.com:** Sergey Gorshkov (cra). **136-137 TurboSquid:** kasiopy. **136 Alamy Stock Photo:** Ralf Liebhold (cra); Then Chih Wey / Xinhua (tl); Southmind (cr). **Dreamstime.com:** Harry Collins (tr). **137 Alamy Stock Photo:** Realimage (crb); Wild Wonders of Europe / Geslin / Nature Picture Library (tl). **Dreamstime.com:** Carolina Garcia Aranda (cr); Susan Sheldon (cra). **naturepl.com:** Steve Gettle (clb). **SuperStock:** Jaymi Heimbuch / Minden Pictures (cla). **140-141 Getty Images:** by wildestanimal. **144 naturepl.com:** Piotr Naskrecki (bl). **146 Alamy Stock Photo:** Peter Maszlen (tr). **147 TurboSquid:** Hum3D (c). **148 naturepl.com:** Murray Cooper (bl). **152-153 SuperStock:** Biosphoto. **154 Science Photo Library:** M. H. Sharp (tl). **157 naturepl.com:** Katherine Feng (tc). **158 123RF. com:** Tawatchai Khid-arn (bl). **158-159 Alamy Stock Photo:** Juan Muñoz / age fotostock. **160 Alamy Stock Photo:** Robert Wyatt (cr). **Dreamstime.com:** Bobhilscher (br). **naturepl.com:** D. Parer & E. Parer-Cook (cra); Steve Gettle (b). **161 Alamy Stock Photo:** Gerhard Koertner / Avalon / Photoshot License (clb). **Dreamstime.com:** Ondej Prosický (cr). **naturepl.com:** Tim Laman / Nat Geo Image Collection (tl); Wild Destinations / Asia / China (br). **162-163 Dhritiman Mukherjee. 164 Alamy Stock Photo:** Andrea Izzotti (tc). **FLPA:** Colin Marshall (cl). **164-165 FLPA:** Colin Marshall. **167 Alamy Stock Photo:** ArteSub (bl); Wildestanimal (c); Michael Stubblefield (sea); Michael Nolan / robertharding (b). **Dreamstime. com:** Kevin Knuth / Drknuth (tr)

All other images © Dorling Kindersley

For further information see: **www.dkimages.com**